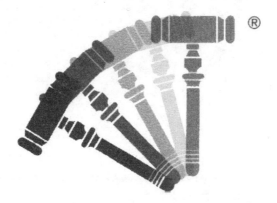

Casenote™ Legal Briefs

GENDER AND LAW

Keyed to
**Bartlett, Harris, and Rhode's
Gender and Law:
Theory, Doctrine, Commentary**

ASPEN

PUBLISHERS

1185 Avenue of the Americas, New York, NY 10036
www.aspenpublishers.com

1 2 3 4 5 6 7 8 9 0

FORMAT FOR THE CASENOTE LEGAL BRIEF

PARTY ID: Quick identification of the relationship between the parties.

NATURE OF CASE: This section identifies the form of action (e.g., breach of contract, negligence, battery), the type of proceeding (e.g., demurrer, appeal from trial court's jury instructions) or the relief sought (e.g., damages, injunction, criminal sanctions).

FACT SUMMARY: This is included to refresh the student's memory and can be used as a quick reminder of the facts.

CONCISE RULE OF LAW: Summarizes the general principle of law that the case illustrates. It may be used for instant recall of the court's holding and for classroom discussion or home review.

FACTS: This section contains all relevant facts of the case, including the contentions of the parties and the lower court holdings. It is written in a logical order to give the student a clear understanding of the case. The plaintiff and defendant are identified by their proper names throughout and are always labeled with a (P) or (D).

ISSUE: The issue is a concise question that brings out the essence of the opinion as it relates to the section of the casebook in which the case appears. Both substantive and procedural issues are included if relevant to the decision.

HOLDING AND DECISION: This section offers a clear and in-depth discussion of the rule of the case and the court's rationale. It is written in easy-to-understand language and answers the issue(s) presented by applying the law to the facts of the case. When relevant, it includes a thorough discussion of the exceptions to the case as listed by the court, any major cites to other cases on point, and the names of the judges who wrote the decisions.

CONCURRENCE / DISSENT: All concurrences and dissents are briefed whenever they are included by the casebook editor.

EDITOR'S ANALYSIS: This last paragraph gives the student a broad understanding of where the case "fits in" with other cases in the section of the book and with the entire course. It is a hornbook-style discussion indicating whether the case is a majority or minority opinion and comparing the principal case with other cases in the casebook. It may also provide analysis from restatements, uniform codes, and law review articles. The editor's analysis will prove to be invaluable to classroom discussion.

QUICKNOTES: Conveniently defines legal terms found in the case and summarizes the nature of any statutes, codes, or rules referred to in the text.

PALSGRAF v. LONG ISLAND R.R. CO.
Injured bystander (P) v. Railroad company (D)
N.Y. Ct. App., 248 N.Y. 339, 162 N.E. 99 (1928).

NATURE OF CASE: Appeal from judgment affirming verdict for plaintiff seeking damages for personal injury.

FACT SUMMARY: Helen Palsgraf (P) was injured on R.R.'s (D) train platform when R.R.'s (D) guard helped a passenger aboard a moving train, causing his package to fall on the tracks. The package contained fireworks which exploded, creating a shock that tipped a scale onto Palsgraf (P).

CONCISE RULE OF LAW: The risk reasonably to be perceived defines the duty to be obeyed.

FACTS: Helen Palsgraf (P) purchased a ticket to Rockaway Beach from R.R. (D) and was waiting on the train platform. As she waited, two men ran to catch a train that was pulling out from the platform. The first man jumped aboard, but the second man, who appeared as if he might fall, was helped aboard by the guard on the train who had kept the door open so they could jump aboard. A guard on the platform also helped by pushing him onto the train. The man was carrying a package wrapped in newspaper. In the process, the man dropped his package, which fell on the tracks. The package contained fireworks and exploded. The shock of the explosion was apparently of great enough strength to tip over some scales at the other end of the platform, which fell on Palsgraf (P) and injured her. A jury awarded her damages, and R.R. (D) appealed.

ISSUE: Does the risk reasonably to be perceived define the duty to be obeyed?

HOLDING AND DECISION: (Cardozo, C.J.) Yes. The risk reasonably to be perceived defines the duty to be obeyed. If there is no foreseeable hazard to the injured party as the result of a seemingly innocent act, the act does not become a tort because it happened to be a wrong as to another. If the wrong was not willful, the plaintiff must show that the act as to her had such great and apparent possibilities of danger as to entitle her to protection. Negligence in the abstract is not enough upon which to base liability. Negligence is a relative concept, evolving out of the common law doctrine of trespass on the case. To establish liability, the defendant must owe a legal duty of reasonable care to the injured party. A cause of action in tort will lie where harm, though unintended, could have been averted or avoided by observance of such a duty. The scope of the duty is limited by the range of danger that a reasonable person could foresee. In this case, there was nothing to suggest from the appearance of the parcel or otherwise that the parcel contained fireworks. The guard could not reasonably have had any warning of a threat to Palsgraf (P), and R.R. (D) therefore cannot be held liable. Judgment is reversed in favor of R.R. (D).

DISSENT: (Andrews, J.) The concept that there is no negligence unless R.R. (D) owes a legal duty to take care as to Palsgraf (P) herself is too narrow. Everyone owes to the world at large the duty of refraining from those acts that may unreasonably threaten the safety of others. If the guard's action was negligent as to those nearby, it was also negligent as to those outside what might be termed the "danger zone." For Palsgraf (P) to recover, R.R.'s (D) negligence must have been the proximate cause of her injury, a question of fact for the jury.

EDITOR'S ANALYSIS: The majority defined the limit of the defendant's liability in terms of the danger that a reasonable person in defendant's situation would have perceived. The dissent argued that the limitation should not be placed on liability, but rather on damages. Judge Andrews suggested that only injuries that would not have happened but for R.R.'s (D) negligence should be compensable. Both the majority and dissent recognized the policy-driven need to limit liability for negligent acts, seeking, in the words of Judge Andrews, to define a framework "that will be practical and in keeping with the general understanding of mankind." The Restatement (Second) of Torts has accepted Judge Cardozo's view.

QUICKNOTES
FORESEEABILITY – The reasonable anticipation that damage is a likely result from certain acts or omissions.

NEGLIGENCE - Failure to exercise that degree of care which a person of ordinary prudence would exercise under similar circumstances.

PROXIMATE CAUSE – Something which in natural and continuous sequence, unbroken by any new intervening cause, produces an event, and without which the injury would not have occurred.

NOTE TO STUDENTS

Aspen Publishers is proud to offer *Casenote Legal Briefs*–continuing thirty years of publishing America's best-selling legal briefs.

Casenote Legal Briefs are designed to help you save time when briefing assigned cases. Organized under convenient headings, they show you how to abstract the basic facts and holdings from the text of the actual opinions handed down by the courts. Used as part of a rigorous study regime, they can help you spend more time analyzing and critiquing points of law than on copying out bits and pieces of judicial opinions into your notebook or outline.

Casenote Legal Briefs should never be used as a substitute for assigned casebook readings. They work best when read as a follow-up to reviewing the underlying opinions themselves. Students who try to avoid reading and digesting the judicial opinions in their casebooks or on-line sources will end up shortchanging themselves in the long run. The ability to absorb, critique, and restate the dynamic and complex elements of case law decisions is crucial to your success in law school and beyond. It cannot be developed vicariously.

Casenote Legal Briefs represent but one of the many offerings in Aspen's Study Aid Timeline, which includes:

- Casenotes *Legal Briefs*
- Emanuel *Outlines*
- *Examples & Explanations* Series
- *Introduction to Law* Series
- Emanuel *Law in A Flash* Flashcards
- Emanuel *CrunchTime* Series

Each of these series is designed to provide you with easy-to-understand explanations of complex points of law. Each volume offers guidance on the principles of legal analysis and, consulted regularly, will hone your ability to spot relevant issues. We have titles that will help you prepare for class, prepare for your exams, and enhance your general comprehension of the law along the way.

To find out more about Aspen Study Aid publications, visit us on-line at www.aspenpublishers.com or e-mail us at legaledu@aspenpubl.com. We'll be happy to assist you.

Free access to Briefs and Updates on-line!

Download the cases you want in your notes or outlines using the full cut-and-paste feature accompanying our on-line briefs. On-line briefs will also contain the latest updates. Please fill out this form for full access to these useful features. No photocopies of this form will be accepted.

① **Name:** _____ **Phone: (____)** _____

Address: _____ **Apt.:** _____

City: _____ **State:** _____ **ZIP Code:** _____

Law School: _____ **Year (circle one):** **1st   2nd   3rd**

② **Cut out the UPC found on the lower left-hand corner of the back cover of this book. Staple the UPC inside this box. Only the original UPC from the book cover will be accepted. (No photocopies or store stickers are allowed.)**

> **Attach UPC inside this box.**

③ **E-mail:** _____ **(Print LEGIBLY or you may not get access!**

④ **Title (course subject) of this book** _____

⑤ **Used with which casebook (provide author's name):** _____

⑥ **Mail the completed form to:**   Aspen Publishers, Inc.
Legal Education Division
Casenote On-line Access
1185 Avenue of the Americas
New York, NY 10036

I understand that on-line access is granted solely to the purchaser of this book for the academic year in which it was purchased. Any other usage is not authorized and will result in immediate termination of access. Sharing of codes is strictly prohibited.

_____

Signature

Upon receipt of this completed form, you will be e-mailed codes so that you may access the Briefs and Updates for this Casenote Legal Brief. On-line Briefs and Updates may not be available for all titles. For a full list of available titles please check www.aspenpublishers.com/casenotes.

HOW TO BRIEF A CASE

A. DECIDE ON A FORMAT AND STICK TO IT

Structure is essential to a good brief. It enables you to arrange systematically the related parts that are scattered throughout most cases, thus making manageable and understandable what might otherwise seem to be an endless and unfathomable sea of information. There are, of course, an unlimited number of formats that can be utilized. However, it is best to find one that suits your needs and stick to it. Consistency breeds both efficiency and the security that when called upon you will know where to look in your brief for the information you are asked to give.

Any format, as long as it presents the essential elements of a case in an organized fashion, can be used. Experience, however, has led *Casenotes* to develop and utilize the following format because of its logical flow and universal applicability.

NATURE OF CASE: This is a brief statement of the legal character and procedural status of the case (e.g., "Appeal of a burglary conviction").

There are many different alternatives open to a litigant dissatisfied with a court ruling. The key to determining which one has been used is to discover *who is asking this court for what.*

This first entry in the brief should be kept as *short as possible.* The student should use the court's terminology if the student understands it. But since jurisdictions vary as to the titles of pleadings, the best entry is the one that apprises the student of who wants what in this proceeding, not the one that sounds most like the court's language.

CONCISE RULE OF LAW: A statement of the general principle of law that the case illustrates (e.g., "An acceptance that varies any term of the offer is considered a rejection and counteroffer").

Determining the rule of law of a case is a procedure similar to determining the issue of the case. Avoid being fooled by red herrings; there may be a few rules of law mentioned in the case excerpt, but usually only one is *the* rule with which the casebook editor is concerned. The techniques used to locate the issue, described below, may also be utilized to find the rule of law. Generally, your best guide is simply the chapter heading. It is a clue to the point the casebook editor seeks to make and should be kept in mind when reading every case in the respective section.

FACTS: A synopsis of only the essential facts of the case, i.e., those bearing upon or leading up to the issue.

The facts entry should be a short statement of the events and transactions that led one party to initiate legal proceedings against another in the first place. While some cases conveniently state the salient facts at the beginning of the decision, in other instances they will have to be culled from hiding places throughout the text, even from concurring and dissenting opinions. Some of the "facts" will often be in dispute and should be so noted. Conflicting evidence may be briefly pointed up. "Hard" facts must be included. Both must be *relevant* in order to be listed in the facts entry. It is impossible to tell what is relevant until the entire case is read, as the ultimate determination of the rights and liabilities of the parties may turn on something buried deep in the opinion.

The facts entry should never be longer than one to three *short* sentences.

It is often helpful to identify the role played by a party in a given context. For example, in a construction contract case the identification of a party as the "contractor" or "builder" alleviates the need to tell that that party was the one who was supposed to have built the house.

It is always helpful, and a good general practice, to identify the "plaintiff" and the "defendant." This may seem elementary and uncomplicated, but, especially in view of the creative editing practiced by some casebook editors, it is sometimes a difficult or even impossible task. Bear in mind that the *party presently* seeking something from this court may not be the plaintiff, and that sometimes only the cross-claim of a defendant is treated in the excerpt. Confusing or misaligning the parties can ruin your analysis and understanding of the case.

ISSUE: A statement of the general legal question answered by or illustrated in the case. For clarity, the issue is best put in the form of a question capable of a "yes" or "no" answer. In reality, the issue is simply the Concise Rule of Law put in the form of a question (e.g., "May an offer be accepted by performance?").

The major problem presented in discerning what is *the* issue in the case is that an opinion usually purports to raise and answer several questions. However, except for rare cases, only one such question is really the issue in the case. Collateral issues not necessary to the resolution of the matter in controversy are handled by the court by language known as *"obiter dictum"* or merely *"dictum."* While dicta may be included later in the brief, it has no place under the issue heading.

To find the issue, the student again asks *who wants what* and then goes on to ask *why did that party succeed or fail in getting it.* Once this is determined, the "why" should be turned into a question.

The complexity of the issues in the cases will vary, but in all cases a single-sentence question should sum up the issue. *In a few cases,* there will be two, or even more rarely, three issues of equal importance to the resolution of the case. Each should be expressed in a single-sentence question.

Since many issues are resolved by a court in coming to a final disposition of a case, the casebook editor will reproduce the portion of the opinion containing the issue or issues most relevant to the area of law under scrutiny. A noted law professor gave this advice: "Close the book; look at the title on the cover." Chances are, if it is Property, the student need not concern himself with whether, for example, the federal government's treatment of the plaintiff's land really raises a federal question sufficient to support jurisdiction on this ground in federal court.

The same rule applies to chapter headings designating sub-areas within the subjects. They tip the student off as to what the text is designed to teach. The cases are arranged in a casebook to show a progression or development of the law, so that the preceding cases may also help.

It is also most important to remember to *read the notes and questions* at the end of a case to determine what the editors wanted the student to have gleaned from it.

HOLDING AND DECISION: This section should succinctly explain the rationale of the court in arriving at its decision. In capsulizing the "reasoning" of the court, it should always include an application of the general rule or rules of law to the specific facts of the case. Hidden justifications come to light in this entry; the reasons for the state of the law, the public policies, the biases and prejudices, those considerations that influence the justices' thinking and, ultimately, the outcome of the case. At the end, there should be a short indication of the disposition or procedural resolution of the case (e.g., "Decision of the trial court for Mr. Smith (P) reversed").

The foregoing format is designed to help you "digest" the reams of case material with which you will be faced in your law school career. Once mastered by practice, it will place at your fingertips the information the authors of your casebooks have sought to impart to you in case-by-case illustration and analysis.

B. BE AS ECONOMICAL AS POSSIBLE IN BRIEFING CASES

Once armed with a format that encourages succinctness, it is as important to be economical with regard to the time spent on the actual reading of the case as it is to be economical in the writing of the brief itself. This does not mean "skimming" a case. Rather, it means reading the case with an "eye" trained to recognize into which "section" of your brief a particular passage or line fits and having a system for quickly and precisely marking the case so that the passages fitting any one particular part of the brief can be easily identified and brought together in a concise and accurate manner when the brief is actually written.

It is of no use to simply repeat everything in the opinion of the court; the student should only record enough information to trigger his or her recollection of what the court said. Nevertheless, an accurate statement of the "law of the case," i.e., the legal principle applied to the facts, is absolutely essential to class preparation and to learning the law under the case method.

To that end, it is important to develop a "shorthand" that you can use to make margin notations. These notations will tell you at a glance in which section of the brief you will be placing that particular passage or portion of the opinion.

Some students prefer to underline all the salient portions of the opinion (with a pencil or colored underliner marker), making marginal notations as they go along. Others prefer the color-coded method of underlining, utilizing different colors of markers to underline the salient portions of the case, each separate color being used to represent a different section of the brief. For example, blue underlining could be used for passages relating to the concise rule of law, yellow for those relating to the issue, and green for those relating to the holding and decision, etc. While it has its advocates, the color-coded method can be confusing and time-consuming (all that time spent on changing colored markers). Furthermore, it can interfere with the continuity and concentration many students deem essential to the reading of a case for maximum comprehension. In the end, however, it is a matter of personal preference and style. Just remember, whatever method you use, underlining must be used sparingly or its value is lost.

For those who take the marginal notation route, an efficient and easy method is to go along underlining the key portions of the case and placing in the margin alongside them the following "markers" to indicate where a particular passage or line "belongs" in the brief you will write:

N   (NATURE OF CASE)
CR   (CONCISE RULE OF LAW)
I   (ISSUE)
HC   (HOLDING AND DECISION, relates to the CONCISE RULE OF LAW behind the decision)
HR   (HOLDING AND DECISION, gives the RATIONALE or reasoning behind the decision)
HA   (HOLDING AND DECISION, APPLIES the general principle(s) of law to the facts of the case to
         arrive at the decision)

Remember that a particular passage may well contain information necessary to more than one part of your brief, in which case you simply note that in the margin. If you are using the color-coded underlining method instead of margin notation, simply make asterisks or checks in the margin next to the passage in question in the colors that indicate the additional sections of the brief where it might be utilized.

The economy of utilizing "shorthand" in marking cases for briefing can be maintained in the actual brief writing process itself by utilizing "law student shorthand" within the brief. There are many commonly used words and phrases for which abbreviations can be substituted in your briefs (and in your class notes also). You can develop abbreviations that are personal to you and which will save you a lot of time. A reference list of briefing abbreviations will be found elsewhere in this book.

C. USE BOTH THE BRIEFING PROCESS AND THE BRIEF AS A LEARNING TOOL

Now that you have a format and the tools for briefing cases efficiently, the most important thing is to make the time spent in briefing profitable to you and to make the most advantageous use of the briefs you create. Of course, the briefs are invaluable for classroom reference when you are called upon to explain or analyze a particular case. However, they are also useful in reviewing for exams. A quick glance at the fact summary should bring the case to mind, and a rereading of the concise rule of law should enable you to go over the underlying legal concept in your mind, how it was applied in that particular case, and how it might apply in other factual settings.

As to the value to be derived from engaging in the briefing process itself, there is an immediate benefit that arises from being forced to sift through the essential facts and reasoning from the court's opinion and to succinctly express them in your own words in your brief. The process ensures that you understand the case and the point that it illustrates, and that means you will be ready to absorb further analysis and information brought forth in class. It also ensures you will have something to say when called upon in class. The briefing process helps develop a mental agility for getting to the *gist* of a case and for identifying, expounding on, and applying the legal concepts and issues found there. Of most immediate concern, that is the mental process on which you must rely in taking law school examinations. Of more lasting concern, it is also the mental process upon which a lawyer relies in serving his clients and in making his living.

ABBREVIATIONS FOR BRIEFING

acceptance	acp
affirmed	aff
answer	ans
assumption of risk	a/r
attorney	atty
beyond a reasonable doubt	b/r/d
bona fide purchaser	BFP
breach of contract	br/k
cause of action	c/a
common law	c/l
Constitution	Con
constitutional	con
contract	K
contributory negligence	c/n
cross	x
cross-complaint	x/c
cross-examination	x/ex
cruel and unusual punishment	c/u/p
defendant	D
dismissed	dis
double jeopardy	d/j
due process	d/p
equal protection	e/p
equity	eq
evidence	ev
exclude	exc
exclusionary rule	exc/r
felony	f/n
freedom of speech	f/s
good faith	g/f
habeas corpus	h/c
hearsay	hr
husband	H
in loco parentis	ILP
injunction	inj
inter vivos	I/v
joint tenancy	j/t
judgment	judgt
jurisdiction	jur
last clear chance	LCC
long-arm statute	LAS
majority view	maj
meeting of minds	MOM
minority view	min
Miranda warnings	Mir/w
Miranda rule	Mir/r
negligence	neg
notice	ntc
nuisance	nus
obligation	ob
obscene	obs

offer	O
offeree	OE
offeror	OR
ordinance	ord
pain and suffering	p/s
parol evidence	p/e
plaintiff	P
prima facie	p/f
probable cause	p/c
proximate cause	px/c
real property	r/p
reasonable doubt	r/d
reasonable man	r/m
rebuttable presumption	rb/p
remanded	rem
res ipsa loquitur	RIL
respondeat superior	r/s
Restatement	RS
reversed	rev
Rule Against Perpetuities	RAP
search and seizure	s/s
search warrant	s/w
self-defense	s/d
specific performance	s/p
statute of limitations	S/L
statute of frauds	S/F
statute	S
summary judgment	s/j
tenancy in common	t/c
tenancy at will	t/w
tenant	t
third party	TP
third party beneficiary	TPB
transferred intent	TI
unconscionable	uncon
unconstitutional	unconst
undue influence	u/e
Uniform Commercial Code	UCC
unilateral	uni
vendee	VE
vendor	VR
versus	v
void for vagueness	VFV
weight of the evidence	w/e
weight of authority	w/a
wife	W
with	w/
within	w/i
without prejudice	w/o/p
without	w/o
wrongful death	wr/d

TABLE OF CASES

Continued on next page.

CHAPTER 1
FOUNDATIONS OF WOMEN'S LEGAL SUBORDINATION

QUICK REFERENCE RULES OF LAW

1. **Legal Subordination..** A common law rule, requiring a married woman to adopt her husband's surname, is constitutional and not in violation of the Equal Protection Clause of the Fourteenth Amendment. (Forbush v. Wallace)

2. **Loss of Property and Contract Rights.** Upon marriage, legal title and the absolute right to a woman's property vests in her husband. (Potts v. Merrit & Potts)

3. **Loss of Property and Contract Rights.** Any services rendered by a wife in her home on behalf of her husband are not on her sole and separate account and do not entitle her to compensation. (Coleman v. Burr)

4. **Excluding Women from the Professions.** The granting of a license to practice law is governed by state law and does not constitute a privilege of United States citizenship. (Bradwell v. Illinois)

5. **Excluding Women from the Professions.** A woman is prohibited from admission to the state bar. (In re Goodell)

6. **Excluding Women from the Professions.** A woman's physical structure and the proper discharge of her maternal functions justify special legislation restricting her employment conditions. (Muller v. Oregon)

7. **Loss of Physical Autonomy.** A court may not convict a husband for moderate correction of his wife without provocation. (State v. Rhodes)

8. **Loss of Physical Autonomy.** A slave may not validly enter a contract of marriage. (State v. Samuel, A Slave)

9. **Controlling Women Through the Regulation of Sexual Norms.** A state statute prohibiting miscegenation does not violate the Constitution of the United States because states have the power to regulate marriage between their citizens. (In re Estate of Fred Paquet, Deceased)

10. **Excluding Women from the Public Sphere of Full Citizenship.** A statute providing that an American woman who marries a foreigner takes the nationality of her husband is constitutional because marriage is voluntarily entered into with knowledge of its consequences. (MacKenzie v. Hare)

11. **Excluding Women from the Public Sphere of Full Citizenship.** The law does not require that a woman be entitled to be tried before a jury of her peers. (United States v. Anthony)

12. **Excluding Women from the Public Sphere of Full Citizenship.** The adoption of the Fourteenth Amendment did not add the right to vote to the privileges and immunities of citizenship. (Minor v. Happersett)

FORBUSH v. WALLACE
Driver's license applicant (P) v. Agency official (D)
341 F. Supp. 217 (M.D. Ala. 1971).

NATURE OF CASE: Class action suit challenging a state agency regulation.

FACT SUMMARY: Forbush (P) brought a class action suit to challenge the Alabama Department of Public Safety's (D) unwritten regulation prohibiting female applicants for a driver's license from being issued those licenses in their maiden names.

CONCISE RULE OF LAW: A common law rule requiring a married woman to adopt her husband's surname is constitutional and not in violation of the Equal Protection Clause of the Fourteenth Amendment.

FACTS: Forbush (P), a married woman, sought to obtain an Alabama driver's license in her maiden name. The Department of Public Safety (D) refused to issue the license in other than her married name. Forbush (P) commenced a class action suit challenging that practice by the Department (D) as well as the adoption of a common law rule that a married woman's legal name was her husband's surname.

ISSUE: Is a common law rule requiring a married woman to adopt her husband's surname constitutional and not in violation of the Equal Protection Clause of the Fourteenth Amendment?

HOLDING AND DECISION: [Per curiam.] Yes. A common law rule requiring a married woman to adopt her husband's surname is constitutional and not in violation of the Equal Protection Clause of the Fourteenth Amendment. A law does not violate the Constitution, even if it is discriminatory, if the state can show that the law has a rational basis in furtherance of a legitimate state interest. The State (D) in this case advances several legitimate interests for a rule requiring a wife to adopt her husband's surname as a matter of law. First, the Department (D) requires that all applicants for a driver's license be issued that license in his or her legal name. That requirement is necessary to permit the department to effectively administer the issuance of licenses and to permit the public to continue to rely on the driver's license as a means of identification. Second, the custom of the wife's adopting her husband's surname upon marriage is prevalent in most societies and among the fifty states. Alabama (D) has a legitimate interest in maintaining uniformity among the states. Last, the implementation of such a change in the State's (D) system of issuing driver's licenses would incur substantial costs and administrative inconvenience. Moreover, a married woman has available the alternative of submitting an application to a probate court to legally change her name. For the foregoing reasons, the law is constitutional.

EDITOR'S ANALYSIS: Note that the court invokes a balancing test in order to weigh the interests of married women against the interests of the state. The court concluded that the administrative inconvenience and costs associated with the implementation of reform in the issuance of driver's licenses significantly outweighed the harm posed to unmarried women by the regulation. Administrative convenience is generally recognized as a permissible basis in support of an allegedly unconstitutional regulation.

QUICKNOTES
DE MINIMIS - Insignificant; trivial; not of sufficient significance to resort to legal action.

NOTES:

2

POTTS v. MERRIT & POTTS

Slave-owning wife (P) v.
Vendee (D) and Husband (D)
Ky. Sup. Ct., 53 Ky. (14B. Mon.) 406 (1854).

NATURE OF CASE: Action to recover personal property.

FACT SUMMARY: Priscilla Potts (P) sought to enforce a verbal pre-nuptial agreement entered into with her husband, whereby she was permitted to retain title and the power of disposition over her slaves.

CONCISE RULE OF LAW: Upon marriage, legal title and the absolute right to a woman's property vests in her husband.

FACTS: Priscilla Potts (P) owned several slaves. After she married, her husband Jonathan sold the slaves to Merrit (D). Priscilla (P) sought to enforce a verbal agreement she entered into with Jonathan (D) prior to their marriage. Pursuant to that agreement, Priscilla (P) was to continue to retain title and the power of disposition over her slaves.

ISSUE: Upon marriage, does legal title and the absolute right to a woman's property vest in her husband?

HOLDING AND DECISION: (Hise, J.) Yes. Upon marriage, legal title and the absolute right to a woman's property vests in her husband. Thus, a woman may not legally maintain an action against either her husband or a third party for the recovery of her pre-marital property. Had the sale of the slaves by Jonathan (D) to Merrit (D) been procured as a result of fraud or incapacity, then Priscilla (P) would have a right to seek to void the contract. While Jonathan (D) is still living, however, Priscilla (P) has no right to maintain such an action. Priscilla (P) contends that the adoption of a will, by which Priscilla (P) devised the slaves to her brother, demonstrates that Jonathan (D) recognized her rights of disposition over those slaves. However, that will can not legally divest Jonathan (D) of his property rights in the slaves during his lifetime. Moreover, the will was fully revocable, and Jonathan (D) impliedly revoked the document upon his sale of the slaves to Merrit (D) and expressly revoked it in writing. Action dismissed.

EDITOR'S ANALYSIS: Under the common law concept of coverture, a husband and wife were considered one person under the law upon marriage. Pursuant to that doctrine, the woman's legal rights were vested in her husband for the duration of the marriage. Since the husband and the wife were legally considered one person, the husband could not convey property to, or enter into contracts with, his wife. In addition, the marriage had the legal effect of voiding all contracts entered into by the spouses prior to the marriage.

QUICKNOTES

FEME COVERT - A woman who is married.

DEVISE - The conferring of a gift of real or personal property by means of a testamentary instrument.

COVERTURE - The former common law rule precluding a married woman from possessing property not subject to her husband's control.

NOTES:

COLEMAN v. BURR
Creditor (P) v. Debtor (D)
N.Y. Ct. of App., 93 N.Y. 17 (1883).

NATURE OF CASE: Appeal from reinstatement of an action to set aside a deed.

FACT SUMMARY: Burr's (D) creditors sought to set aside two conveyances made by Burr (D) of a sixty-two acre tract of land on the basis that it was intended to defraud his creditors.

CONCISE RULE OF LAW: Any services rendered by a wife in her home on behalf of her husband are not on her sole and separate account and do not entitle her to compensation.

FACTS: Burr (D) lived on a tract of sixty-two acres of land with his wife, Ellen (D), their children, and his mother. Burr (D) agreed to support his mother, who was paralyzed, in consideration for twenty-six acres of the tract. Ellen (D) performed most of the duties necessary to care for Burr's (D) mother. The couple agreed that Ellen (D) would be compensated for such services in the sum of five dollars per week. Ellen (D) continued to render such services to Burr's (D) mother for eight years, and the compensation due to her amounted to $2,175. Burr (D) and Ellen subsequently conveyed the sixty-two acres to Smith (D) for one dollar, who reconveyed the land to Ellen (D) for one dollar. Prior to this transaction, Burr (D) had incurred several other debts for which judgments had been obtained and were unsatisfied. This action was brought by Coleman (P) and others to set aside those deeds on the basis that they were intended to defraud Burr's (D) creditors. The referee held that the deeds were valid in consideration of the sum due to Ellen (D) and thus were not fraudulent or void. The complaint was dismissed. Coleman (P) appealed. The appellate court reversed, and Burr (D) appealed.

ISSUE: Are any services rendered by a wife in her home on behalf of her husband on her sole and separate account, entitling her to compensation?

HOLDING AND DECISION: (Earl, J.) No. Any services rendered by a wife in her home on behalf of her husband are not on her sole and separate account and do not entitle her to compensation. At common law, the general rule was that any services rendered by a wife were on behalf of her husband and she was thus prohibited from contracting with her husband therefor. Recent legislation regarding married women's marital property granted women the authority to control their own property upon marriage. Additional legislation permitted women to conduct business and to perform services on her sole and separate account. The earnings from these activities were to remain her separate property, no longer subject to her husband's control. The purpose of these statutes, however, was to protect the woman from abuse by her husband and not to relieve her of her marital duties. Here Ellen (D) performed the tasks of caring for Burr's (D) mother. These duties were performed on account of Burr's (D) obligation to support his mother and were in the nature of marital duties for which Ellen (D) was not entitled to receive compensation. Affirmed.

EDITOR'S ANALYSIS: Under the common law, there existed a presumption that the husband and wife comprised one person for purposes of the law. Under the "doctrine of marital unity" or "coverture," the husband and wife were precluded from entering into contracts with each other. The wife was particularly hindered in that the husband assumed all management and control of her personal property upon marriage. States began enacting legislation permitting women to control their own property so as to avoid abuse by the husband. The courts and legislature responded by imposing restrictions in regard to compensation for the wife's performance of her household duties.

QUICKNOTES

CONSIDERATION - Value given by one party in exchange for performance, or a promise to perform, by another party.

MARRIED WOMEN'S PROPERTY ACT - secured to women the separate and independent control of their property.

NOTES:

BRADWELL v. ILLINOIS

Bar applicant (P) v. State of Illinois (D)

83 U.S. (16 Wall.) 130 (1872).

NATURE OF CASE: Appeal from state court denial of an application to practice law.

FACT SUMMARY: Bradwell (P) sought review of an Illinois Supreme Court decision denying her application to practice law In that state on the basis that she was a married woman.

CONCISE RULE OF LAW: The granting of a license to practice law is governed by state law and does not constitute a privilege of United States citizenship.

FACTS: Bradwell (P) applied to the Illinois Supreme Court for a license to practice law. A state statute prohibited persons from practicing as an attorney without having obtained a license from at least two supreme court justices. Bradwell's (P) application was denied on the basis that she was a married woman. Bradwell (P) appealed.

ISSUE: Is the granting of a license to practice law governed by state law?

HOLDING AND DECISION: (Miller, J.) Yes. The granting of a license to practice law is governed by state law and does not constitute a privilege of United States citizenship. Affirmed.

CONCURRENCE: (Bradley, J.) Bradwell (P) claimed that the Fourteenth Amendment guarantees to women the right to pursue lawful employment for gain as a privilege of United States citizenship. The right to engage in any type of employment whatsoever has not been established as one of the fundamental privileges and immunities. Rather, the law, as well as nature, has necessarily dictated that women be restricted to performing certain functions, primarily the maintenance of the family home. The importance of maintaining family harmony was the basis for the common law premise that the man and woman comprise a single unit. It is the function of the state legislature and not the courts to prescribe what positions may be discharged by the particular gender.

EDITOR'S ANALYSIS: The concurrence recognized that a woman may engage in gainful employment, but restricted the scope of such employment to those occupations as may be prescribed by the state. The concurrence cited as the basis for its opinion the common law doctrine of "coverture," whereby the woman was considered to have no separate legal identity from that of her husband. The Court upheld the doctrine of coverture as the prevailing law in the majority of states despite the enactment of the Fourteenth Amendment.

QUICKNOTES

FOURTEENTH AMENDMENT - declares that no state shall make or enforce any law which shall abridge the privileges and immunities of citizens of the United States.

COVERTURE - The former common law rule precluding a married woman from possessing property not subject to her husband's control.

NOTES:

IN RE GOODELL
Bar applicant
Wis. Sup. Ct., 39 Wis. 232 (1875).

NATURE OF CASE: Application for admission to the state bar.

FACT SUMMARY: Goodell's (P) application for admission to the Wisconsin state bar was the first application by a woman in that state.

CONCISE RULE OF LAW: A woman is prohibited from admission to the state bar.

FACTS: Goodell's (P) application for admission to the Wisconsin state bar was the first application by a woman in that state.

ISSUE: Is a woman prohibited from admission to the state bar?

HOLDING AND DECISION: (Ryan, C.J.) Yes. A woman is prohibited from admission to the state bar. This case presented an issue of first instance in this court. Neither statutory law nor the common law provides for the admission of a woman to practice law in Wisconsin. Nature dictates that the woman care for the family and tend to the household duties. While a woman is not absolutely prohibited from seeking gainful employment, such employment should be limited to those pursuits more suitable to a woman's nature. A woman is not suited for the rigors and conflicts presented in the courtroom. Motion denied.

EDITOR'S ANALYSIS: Note that the court takes a paternalistic role in prohibiting women from admission to the bar. The court was of the opinion that the matters with which the legal profession deals was not suitable for women. It suggested that permitting them to participate in such matters would have a negative effect on public morality.

QUICKNOTES
REDUCTIO AD ABSURDUM - The refuting of a legal argument by demonstrating its absurdity.

NOTES:

MULLER v. OREGON

Laundry owner (D) v. State of Oregon (P)

208 U.S. 412 (1908).

NATURE OF CASE: Writ of error from state supreme court decision convicting defendant of a violation of state labor law.

FACT SUMMARY: Muller (D) contended that a state statute prohibiting women from working in a factory or similar establishment for longer than ten hours per day was unconstitutional on freedom to contract and equal protection grounds.

CONCISE RULE OF LAW: A woman's physical structure and the proper discharge of her maternal functions justify special legislation restricting her employment conditions.

FACTS: An Oregon (P) state law prohibited women from working in any factory or similar establishment for longer than ten hours per day. Muller (D) was charged with violating that statute on the basis that he required Mrs. Gotcher to work in his factory in excess of the ten-hour limit. The trial court found Muller (D) guilty and fined him $10. Muller (D) appealed, arguing that the law interfered with women's right to contract and was not a valid exercise of the police power of the State (P). The state supreme court affirmed. The U.S. Supreme Court granted Muller's (D) petition for certiori.

ISSUE: Does a woman's physical structure justify special legislation restricting her employment conditions?

HOLDING AND DECISION: (Brewer, J.) Yes. A woman's physical structure and the proper discharge of her maternal functions justify special legislation restricting her employment conditions. Women, regardless of their marital status, possess equal contractual and personal rights as men. This Court held in Lochner v. New York, 198 U.S. 45 (1905), that a similar law restricting the hours of labor a man may work in a bakery was unconstitutional in violation of the individual's right to contract. Muller (D) contended that the Court's holding in that case resolves the issue presented in this matter. That result, however, would presume that neither sex requires a different rule in respect to permissible working hours. A woman's physical nature and maternal functions requires that she receive particular protection from abuse. Thus, the Court may uphold a statute imposing restrictions on such labor that may not be upheld if similarly imposed on a man. A limitation restricting a woman's right to contract regarding the number of hours she may work per day is a proper exercise of legislative discretion and is not unconstitutional. Affirmed.

EDITOR'S ANALYSIS: The movement to shorten the working day was not originally gender based. Rather, it was motivated by the public interest in encouraging a more active and knowledgeable populace. Such restrictions on the permissible working hours of men were initially struck down on the basis that they interfered with the individual's right to contract. Courts were more receptive to laws imposing the same restraints on the permissible hours a woman may work, however, based on the contention that the woman was entitled to special protection based on her maternal functions.

QUICKNOTES

WRIT OF ERROR - A writ issued by an appellate court, ordering a lower court to deliver the record of the case so that it may be reviewed for alleged errors.

SUI JURIS - An individual who is not legally dependent upon another or subject to a legal disability.

NOTES:

STATE v. RHODES

State of North Carolina (P) v. Acquitted wife beater (D)

N.C. Sup. Ct., 61 N.C. 453 (1868).

NATURE OF CASE: Appeal from verdict for defendant in assault and battery case.

FACT SUMMARY: The State (P) appealed from the trial judge's holding that Rhodes (D) was not guilty of committing an assault and battery upon his wife.

CONCISE RULE OF LAW: A court may not convict a husband for moderate correction of his wife without provocation.

FACTS: Rhodes (D) was indicted for committing assault and battery upon his wife, Elizabeth. The jury found by special verdict that Rhodes (D) had battered his wife with a switch smaller than his thumb, without provocation; upon these facts, the trial court judge concluded that Rhodes (D) was not guilty as a matter of law. Judgment was entered in favor of Rhodes (D). The State (P) appealed.

ISSUE: May a court convict a husband for moderate correction of his wife without provocation?

HOLDING AND DECISION: (Reade, J.) No. A court may not court convict a husband for moderate correction of his wife without provocation. The court will not interfere in matters of family government, unless permanent or malicious injury is threatened or inflicted or the husband grossly abuses his powers. Imposing an element of provocation would be an impossible standard to prove. The husband does not have a right to strike his wife; however, the court will not interfere when the resulting injury is minimal. Affirmed.

EDITOR'S ANALYSIS: Under the common law, the husband was permitted to give his wife "moderate correction." The rationale behind this doctrine was that since the husband was liable for his wife's actions, he should therefore have the authority to discipline her. The husband was permitted, however, to utilize only that force that was reasonable under the circumstances and was prohibited from administering excessive violence.

NOTES:

STATE v. SAMUEL, A SLAVE

State of North Carolina (P) v. Convicted murderer (D)

N.C. Sup. Ct., 19 N.C. 177 (1836).

NATURE OF CASE: Appeal from a conviction for first degree murder.

FACT SUMMARY: Samuel (D), a slave, appealed from his conviction for the murder of another slave on the basis that his wife improperly testified against him at trial.

CONCISE RULE OF LAW: A slave may not validly enter a contract of marriage.

FACTS: Samuel (D), a slave, was arrested for the murder of another slave. Mima, Samuel's (D) wife and the only witness to the crime, was called to testify. The defense objected. Mima's owner, Lea, testified that Samuel (D) and Mima had lived together for ten years. Lea further testified that she had overheard an argument between Samuel (D) and Mima, after which she saw Samuel (D) leave. Lea instructed Samuel (D) not to return until he had an order from his master to retrieve his belongings. The murder victim subsequently asked Lea for permission to take Mima as his wife. Lea granted that permission. The defense objected to Mima's competency to testify. The trial judge overruled the objection. Samuel (D) was convicted of first degree murder. Samuel (D) appealed.

ISSUE: May a slave validly enter a contract of marriage?

HOLDING AND DECISION: (Ruffin, C.J.) No. A slave may not validly enter a contract of marriage. The defense argued that Mima was prohibited from testifying against Samuel (D) on the basis that she was his wife, and therefore the rules of evidence precluded the allowance of her testimony against him. Any person who is not expressly excluded by law should be permitted to present testimony. The rule prohibiting the testimony of a husband or wife against the other is based on the public's interest in maintaining harmony in the family unit. Such exclusion of testimony necessarily depends upon the existence of a legal marriage contract. The common law does not recognize a couple as husband and wife merely by the fact that they have cohabitated for a specified period of time, thus entitling them to the legal privileges of the marital status. Likewise, there is no such privilege for slaves, since they are prohibited from validly entering into a contract for marriage. Since Mima was never the wife of Samuel (D) as a matter of law, her testimony against him was permissible. Affirmed.

EDITOR'S ANALYSIS: The defense argued that the standard should be whether or not the parties consented to the marital contract, and thus a contract could be inferred from their words or actions. The court rejected that argument, however, on the basis that the legal incidents of marriage may not be granted without an express marital contract. The general rule was that a slave was precluded from entering into contracts by virtue of the reason that he did not possess free consent. Thus, the court was precluded from granting the slaves such privileges merely on the basis of their cohabitation.

QUICKNOTES

PERSONS SUI JURIS - An individual who is not legally dependent upon another or subject to a legal disability.

MARRIAGE DE JURE - A marriage that complies with all legal requirements for a valid marriage.

PRETERMITTED - Omitted; usually refers to an heir who is unintentionally omitted from a testator's will.

CONCUBINAGE - Refers to a situation in which a woman and man cohabitate without being legally married.

NOTES:

IN RE ESTATE OF FRED PAQUET, DECEASED
Widow of deceased (P) v. Brother of deceased (D)
200 P. 911 (Oregon, 1921).

NATURE OF CASE: Appeal to determine proper administrator of a will.

FACT SUMMARY: Fred Paquet's brother, John (D), filed a petition to have Paquet's widow, Ophelia (P), removed as the administrator of Fred's will on the grounds that she was a full-blooded Indian and, therefore, their marriage was null and void. A lower court removed Ophelia (P) and appointed John (D) as the administrator of Paquet's estate. Ophelia (P) appealed to the Supreme Court of Oregon.

CONCISE RULE OF LAW: A state statute prohibiting miscegenation does not violate the Constitution of the United States because states have the power to regulate marriage between their citizens.

FACTS: Ophelia (P) and Fred Paquet were married in Tillamook County, Oregon, according to Indian tribal custom. Under Indian law, the two were considered married. However, Oregon law prohibited the marriage between a white person and a person of having more than one half Indian blood. After Fred died, Ophelia (P) filed a petition to be the administrator of his will. A county court granted her petition. John Paquet (D), Fred's brother, then filed a petition to have Ophelia removed and have himself appointed as the administrator. The Court found in favor of John (D), and Ophelia (P) filed this appeal. In the meantime, a creditor of the estate, Henkle, filed a petition to have John (D) removed and himself appointed based on his claim that John (D) was of unsound mind and of immoral character. The cases were consolidated and reviewed by the Oregon Supreme Court.

ISSUE: Is a state statute prohibiting marriage between a white person and a full-blooded Indian constitutional?

HOLDING AND DECISION: (Bagley, J.) Yes. Oregon state law prohibits miscegenation. A marriage between a white person and a person with Indian blood is null and void. Appellant contends that the state statute prohibiting miscegenation is unconstitutional. All over the country such laws have been attacked on the grounds that they violate the United States Constitution. However, these laws have been universally upheld as the proper exercise of a state's power to control its own citizens.

EDITOR'S ANALYSIS: Ophelia and Fred Paquet had been married for more than thirty years before his death. Miscegenation laws did not prevent their living together and having a marital relationship. The impact of miscegenation laws was that they ultimately controlled the distribution of property. They prevented people of color from obtaining property through marriage. Although Ophelia likely contributed financially to her husband's property throughout the thirty years of their marriage, a white relative was able to obtain it all merely through relying on miscegenation laws.

NOTES:

MACKENZIE v. HARE
Wife of foreigner (P) v. Government agent (D)
239 U.S. 299 (1915).

NATURE OF CASE: Constitutional challenge to statute governing citizenship of women.

FACT SUMMARY: Mackenzie (P) married a citizen of the Kingdom of Great Britain, and then was not allowed to vote because of a Congressional statute providing that an American woman who marries a foreigner takes the nationality of her husband.

CONCISE RULE OF LAW: A statute providing that an American woman who marries a foreigner takes the nationality of her husband is constitutional because marriage is voluntarily entered into with knowledge of its consequences.

FACTS: Mackenzie (P) was born in the United States and lived in California. She married a citizen of the U.K. and the two lived together in California. When Mackenzie (P) went to vote, she was prohibited from doing so because her marriage rendered her a citizen of the U.K. Mackenzie (P) filed this appeal to the Supreme Court of the United States.

ISSUE: Is a statute providing that an American woman who marries a foreigner takes on the nationality of her husband constitutional?

HOLDING AND DECISION: (McKenna, J.) Yes. The appellant argues that the statute at issue is unconstitutional because it is beyond the authority of Congress to deprive her of her citizenship, as it was an incident to her birth in the United States. Mackenzie (P) maintains that her citizenship was a right, privilege and immunity that Congress could not deprive her of except as a punishment for a crime or her voluntary expatriation. The Court acknowledges that a change of citizenship cannot be arbitrarily imposed. However, the law at issue deals with a condition voluntarily entered into. Mackenzie (P) elected to marry a citizen of the U.K. and her decision was tantamount to expatriation.

EDITOR'S ANALYSIS: The United States adopted the English laws with respect to marriage. As a result, the institution of marriage in the United States was based on the premise that a woman, although a citizen, received her rights through her husband. Her obligations to him, therefore, were more significant than her obligations to the state. In this case, Mackenzie's choice of marrying a man from another country necessarily implied her expatriation.

UNITED STATES v. ANTHONY

Federal government (P) v. Suffragist (D)

History of Women's Suffrage, vol. II, 1861-1876 at 688-689 (Stanton, Anthony & Gage, eds., reprint ed. 1985) (1873).

NATURE OF CASE: Trial for violation of federal statute.

FACT SUMMARY: Susan B. Anthony (D) was charged with voting in violation of a federal statute prohibiting multiple voting by white voters for the purpose of weakening black votes.

CONCISE RULE OF LAW: The law does not require that a woman be entitled to be tried before a jury of her peers.

FACTS: Anthony (D) was charged with voting in violation of § 19 of the Civil Rights Act of 1870, a federal statute prohibiting multiple voting by white voters for the purpose of weakening black votes. The case was not submitted to a jury. The judge held Anthony (D) guilty of violating the statute.

ISSUE: Does the law require that a woman be entitled to be tried before a jury of her peers?

HOLDING AND DECISION: (Hunt, J.) No. The law does not require that a woman be entitled to be tried before a jury of her peers. Anthony (D) argued that since no woman was permitted to practice law or sit on a jury, she was nonetheless entitled to be tried by a jury of men. The judge held that the trial was conducted in conformity with the law. Anthony (D) was ordered to pay a fine of $100 and the prosecution's costs.

EDITOR'S ANALYSIS: Note that in the present case, Anthony (D) conceded that she would not be afforded a trial by a jury of her peers, but rather by a jury of only men. Existing law precluded women from performing jury service. Anthony (D) used the occasion to hold forth on her deeply held beliefs regarding man-made, unjust, unconstitutional forms of law that taxed, fined, imprisoned, and hanged women while denying them the right of representation.

QUICKNOTES

CIVIL RIGHTS ACT OF 1870, § 19 - statute intended to prohibit multiple voting by white voters.

NOTES:

MINOR v. HAPPERSETT
Suffragist (P) v. State official (D)
88 U.S.(21 Wall.) 162 (1875).

NATURE OF CASE: Appeal from decision holding a state statute constitutional.

FACT SUMMARY: Mr. and Mrs. Minor (P) challenged the legality of a state statute restricting the right to vote to male citizens as unconstitutional in violation of the Fourteenth Amendment.

CONCISE RULE OF LAW: The adoption of the Fourteenth Amendment did not add the right to vote to the privileges and immunities of citizenship.

FACTS: Mr. and Mrs. Minor (P) challenged the legality of a state statute restricting the right to vote to male citizens as unconstitutional in violation of the Fourteenth Amendment.

ISSUE: Did the adoption of the Fourteenth Amendment add the right to vote to the privileges and immunities of citizenship?

HOLDING AND DECISION: (Waite, C.J.) No. The adoption of the Fourteenth Amendment did not add the right to vote to the privileges and immunities of citizenship. Women have always been entitled to citizenship in the United States and to the privileges and immunities thereof. The passage of the Fourteenth Amendment had no effect as to the rights of women. The Fourteenth Amendment prohibits states from enacting laws that abridge the privileges and immunities of citizenship; however, it does not confer additional rights. While it may have conferred the right to vote on new citizens affected by the Amendment, it does so indirectly through the operation of state law. If the right to vote is such a privilege, then a state law confining that privilege solely to men is unconstitutional and void. Moreover, no state has conferred that right upon all its citizens. If a law denying the right to vote to women citizens is unconstitutional, it is an issue for the legislature and not the Court to resolve. Affirmed.

EDITOR'S ANALYSIS: Mr. and Mrs. Minor (P) raised a novel argument, contending that women as citizens of the United States were entitled to the privileges and immunities thereof and had always been entitled to suffrage as a matter of law. The Court rejected that argument on the basis that the states ware not required to grant an unlimited right to vote to all their citizens. In addition, the Court asserted that had the Framers intended such a result, they would have granted an absolute right to vote as a privilege of citizenship. Since no state at that time had permitted women to vote, the Court declined to grant such a privilege in the present case.

QUICKNOTES

FOURTEENTH AMENDMENT OF THE U.S. CONSTITUTION - declares all persons born or naturalized in the United States and of the state wherein they reside and prohibits states from abridging their privileges and immunities.

FIFTEENTH AMENDMENT - states that the right of citizens of the United States to vote shall not bo doniod on aooount of raoo, oolor, or provious condition of servitude.

NOTES:

2

CHAPTER 2
FORMAL EQUALITY

QUICK REFERENCE RULES OF LAW

1. **The Right to Equal, Individualized Treatment.** The Equal Protection Clause prohibits states from enacting legislation affording different treatment to particular classes of persons based on factors that do not bear a rational relationship to the objective of the statute. (Reed v. Reed)

2. **The Right to Equal, Individualized Treatment.** Gender-based classifications are inherently suspect and subject to strict judicial scrutiny. (Frontiero v. Richardson)

3. **The Right to Equal, Individualized Treatment.** The Equal Protection Clause requires that classifications based on gender must be substantially related to the furtherance of an important state interest. (Orr v. Orr)

4. **The Rights to Equal Group Treatment.** A classification based on sex may only be upheld if it is reasonable and bears a fair and substantial relation to the legislature's objective in providing uniform treatment to similarly situated persons. (Stanton v. Stanton)

5. **The Rights to Equal Group Treatment.** A gender-based classification must be substantially related to the furtherance of an important state interest in order to be constitutionally permissible. (Craig v. Boren)

6. **The Right to Be Free of Indirect Discrimination.** When a gender-neutral law has a disparate impact upon a group of persons that has been the victim of past discrimination, it may be unconstitutional in violation of the Equal Protection Clause. (Personnel Administrator of Massachusetts v. Feeney)

7. **The Equal Pay Act: Formal Equality Paradigm.** The Equal Pay Act guarantees equal pay to men and women who perform equal work in employment that requires an equivalent degree of skill, effort, and responsibility and is performed under similar working conditions. (EEOC v. Madison Community Unit School District No.12)

8. **The Equal Pay Act: Formal Equality Paradigm.** Economic benefits to an employer are a sufficient justification for a wage differential under the Equal Pay Act. (Hodgson v. Robert Hall Clothes, Inc.)

9. **What Is Discrimination "Based on Sex"?** An employer may enact and enforce personal appearance regulations so long as those standards are not invidiously applied. (Craft v. Metromedia, Inc.)

10. **What Is Discrimination "Based on Sex"?** An employer is not liable for a violation of Title VII in making an employment decision if it demonstrates that it would have made the same decision in the absence of a discriminatory intent. (Price Waterhouse v. Hopkins)

11. **What Is Discrimination "Based on Sex"?** When an employer relies on its subjective evaluation of the plaintiff's qualifications as the reason for denying promotion, the plaintiff can prove the reason is unworthy of credence by presenting persuasive comparative evidence that non-members of the protected class were evaluated more favorably. (Ezold v. Wolf, Block, Schorr & Solis-Cohen)

12. **When is Discrimination a "Bona Fide Occupational Qualification"?** In order to establish a prima facie case of discrimination in respect to facially neutral employment standards, a plaintiff must demonstrate that such qualifications result in the selection of employees in a significantly discriminatory manner. (Dothard v. Rawlinson)

13. **When Is Discrimination a "Bona Fide Occupational Qualification"?** An employer may consider sex as a bona fide occupational qualification only when it is reasonably necessary to the continued operation of the business. (Wilson v. Southwest Airlines Co.)

14. **When Is Discrimination a "Bona Fide Occupational Qualification"?.** An employer's implementation of a gender-based, fetal-protection policy constitutes sex discrimination in violation of Title VII, unless the employer can show that sex is a "bona fide occupational qualification." (UAW v. Johnson Controls, Inc.)

15. **State Public Accommodations Laws and First Amendment Associational Freedoms.** An individual's freedom to enter into and carry on intimate or private relationships is a fundamental liberty interest under the First Amendment. (Board of Directors of Rotary International v. Rotary Club of Duarte)

16. **State Public Accommodations Laws and First Amendment Associational Freedoms.** The Unruh Civil Rights Act prohibits arbitrary discrimination on the basis of sex by a business establishment. (Isbister v. Boys' Club of Santa Cruz, Inc.)

REED v. REED

Decedent's mother (P) v. Decedent's father (D)

404 U.S. 71 (1971).

NATURE OF CASE: Review of judgment upholding the constitutional validity of a state statute.

FACT SUMMARY: Sally Reed (P) challenged the constitutional validity of an Idaho state statute granting preference to males over females in the appointment of administrators of intestate estates.

CONCISE RULE OF LAW: The Equal Protection Clause prohibits states from enacting legislation affording different treatment to particular classes of persons based on factors that do not bear a rational relationship to the objective of the statute.

FACTS: Richard Lynn Reed, a minor, died intestate. His adoptive parents had separated prior to his death. His mother, Sally (P), filed a petition in probate court seeking to be appointed as administratix of Richard's estate. His father, Cecil (D), filed a competing petition for appointment as administrator. The probate court held a joint hearing on the petitions and ordered Cecil (D) to be appointed as administrator of the state. The court's decision was based on a state statute providing a preference to males. Idaho Code § 15-312 set forth the classes of persons entitled to administer the estate of a decedent who dies intestate in order of priority. One such class referred to the father or mother of the decedent. Section 15-314, however, provided that in cases in which persons are equally entitled to administration under § 15-312, males must be afforded preference over females. Sally (P) appealed. The state supreme court upheld the statute. The Supreme Court granted review.

ISSUE: Does the Equal Protection Clause prohibit states from enacting legislation affording different treatment to particular classes of persons based on factors that do not bear a rational relationship to the objective of the statute?

HOLDING AND DECISION: (Burger, C.J.) Yes. The Equal Protection Clause prohibits states from enacting legislation affording different treatment to particular classes of persons based on factors that do not bear a rational relationship to the objective of the statute. Here, § 15-314 afforded different treatment to applicants for administration of an intestate estate on the basis of sex. Such a classification is subject to scrutiny by the courts. While the Equal Protection Clause does not absolutely prohibit states from enacting legislation treating different classes of persons in different ways, states may not enact legislation drawing classifications in an arbitrary or unreasonable manner unrelated to the objective of the statute. When a statute draws a distinction between particular classes of persons, such classification must bear a fair and substantial relation to the objective of the statute. The issue here is whether a distinction in the granting of letters of administration to competing applicants on the basis of sex bears a rational relationship to the furtherance of an objective, that the state sought to attain by enacting the statute. The objective advanced by the state supreme court was the efficient resolution of cases in the probate courts. The legislature in achieving that goal, however, made an arbitrary distinction between the sexes in violation of the Equal Protection Clause. Reversed.

EDITOR'S ANALYSIS: At this juncture in gender jurisprudence, the Court begins employing principles used to review civil rights cases in constitutional challenges to discrimination on the basis of sex. The Court also formulates an "intermediate" scrutiny analysis, requiring the classification to be substantially related to the advancement of an important state objective or to be supported by "an exceedingly persuasive justification." This standard of review requires a court to examine the assumptions on which a gender-based distinction is made and to determine whether the classification furthers the proposed justifications.

QUICKNOTES

IDAHO CODE § 15-312 - designates in order of priority the persons who are entitled to administer the estate of one who dies intestate.

IDAHO CODE § 15-314 - provides that if more than one person claims to be equally entitled under § 15-312 to administer, males must be preferred to females.

INTESTATE - To die without leaving a valid testamentary instrument.

NOTES:

FRONTIERO v. RICHARDSON
Female Air Force lieutenant (P) v.
Federal government official (D)
411 U.S. 677 (1973).

NATURE OF CASE: Review of judgment sustaining constitutional validity of federal benefits statutes.

FACT SUMMARY: Frontiero (P), a female lieutenant in the United States Air Force, challenged the validity of a statutory scheme permitting male armed forces members to claim their wives as dependents automatically while not permitting female armed forces members to claim their husbands as dependents unless they were responsible for over one-half of their husband's support.

CONCISE RULE OF LAW: Gender-based classifications are inherently suspect and subject to strict judicial scrutiny.

FACTS: Sharron Frontiero (P), a lieutenant in the United States Air Force, sought increased allowances and benefits, claiming that her husband was a dependent. Frontiero's (P) application was denied on the basis that she had failed to show that he relied on her for one-half of his support pursuant to federal statutes. Existing federal law permitted males to claim their wives as dependents regardless of whether they were in fact dependent on their husbands for any part of their support. Frontiero (P) challenged the validity of the statutes on the basis that they violated the Due Process Clause of the Fifth Amendment. She also sought a permanent injunction to prohibit the enforcement of the statutes and an order to provide her with the same housing and benefits that a male would receive under the law. The district court upheld the statute. Frontiero (P) appealed.

ISSUE: Are gender-based classifications inherently suspect and subject to strict judicial scrutiny?

HOLDING AND DECISION: (Brennan, J.) Yes. Gender-based classifications are inherently suspect and subject to strict judicial scrutiny. Moreover, sex is an immutable characteristic. Laws that draw distinctions between males and females result in the subordination of females as a class without consideration of the individual abilities of its members. Similarly, Congress has recently enacted legislation to remedy discrimination on the basis of sex in the workplace and has recognized through the Equal Rights Amendment that classifications based on gender are inherently suspect. Applying the strict scrutiny standard to the present case, the statutes are invalid. The statutes distinguish between similarly situated males and females solely on the basis of sex. A female member of the armed forces must establish her husband's dependency in order to receive benefits, while a similar burden is not imposed on males. Moreover, the statutes deny benefits to females who provide less than one-half their husband's support, while males may receive such benefits regardless of the amount of support they provide their spouses. Although administrative convenience is an important state interest, when the Court applies strict scrutiny analysis, such an objective does not absolutely sustain a challenged statute. The statutory scheme in the present case violates the Due Process Clause of the Fifth Amendment by affording similarly situated armed forces members different treatment solely on the basis of their sex. Reversed.

CONCURRENCE: (Powell, J.) The Court did not need to characterize sex as an inherently suspect classification subject to strict scrutiny analysis. Congress will resolve the issue in determining whether to ratify the Equal Rights Amendment.

EDITOR'S ANALYSIS: In reviewing the constitutional validity of a discriminatory statute, the Court must first determine whether to invoke an intermediate scrutiny analysis or a strict scrutiny. Pursuant to the intermediate scrutiny analysis, the Court must determine whether the classification is substantially related to the furtherance of an important state interest. This standard differs from the strict scrutiny analysis, which requires the proponent of the validity of the statute to show that the law is necessary for the advancement of a compelling state interest and is the least restrictive alternative.

QUICKNOTES

TITLE 37 U.S.C. § 401 - defines "dependent," with respect to a member of a uniformed service as his spouse; however, a person is not a dependent of a female member unless he is in fact dependent on her for over one-half of his support.

EQUAL RIGHTS AMENDMENT - its passage would have mandated a stricter review of classifications based on sex, but it failed to gain the support of thirty-eight states necessary for adoption.

NOTES:

ORR v. ORR
Husband (D) v. Wife (P)
440 U.S. 268 (1979).

NATURE OF CASE: Review of denial of motion to declare alimony statutes unconstitutional in contempt proceeding.

FACT SUMMARY: William Orr (D) challenged the constitutional validity of Alabama state alimony statutes on the basis that they impermissibly distinguished between males and females in the imposition of support obligations.

CONCISE RULE OF LAW: The Equal Protection Clause requires that classifications based on gender must be substantially related to the furtherance of an important state interest.

FACTS: William (D) and Lillian Orr (P) were divorced in 1974. Alabama alimony statutes provided that husbands, but not wives, may be required to pay alimony. The court ordered William (D) to pay Lillian (P) $1,240 a month in alimony. Lillian (P) commenced contempt proceedings in order to require William (D) to make the payments. William (D) challenged the constitutional validity of the state alimony statutes on the basis that they impermissibly discriminated between men and women. The circuit court denied the motion and held in favor of Lillian (P). William (D) appealed.

ISSUE: Does the Equal Protection Clause require that classifications based on gender must be substantially related to the furtherance of an important state interest?

HOLDING AND DECISION: (Brennan, J.) Yes. The Equal Protection Clause requires that classifications based on gender must be substantially related to the furtherance of an important state interest. This standard of review is equally applicable to statutes that discriminate against males as well as females. Courts have consistently struck down statutes imposing responsibility on the male to provide support for the family on the basis of outdated notions of the male's obligations. In this case, the court of civil appeals stated that the legislature's objective was the financial protection of the wife. This may be interpreted as either providing assistance for spouses on the basis of sex, or as compensating women for past discrimination placing them at a disadvantage in the workplace. While these goals constitute important state interests, it must be determined whether the statute in question substantially furthers those objectives. Both these purposes could be adequately achieved without discriminating between the spouses on the basis of sex. Since the statute already provides for the case-by-case determination of the financial positions of the parties, a gender-neutral alimony statute could be implemented with minimal burden on the state. Moreover, the present statute causes results contrary to the legislature's intent. The statute provides a benefit to financially secure wives who are relieved of the duty to provide alimony payments to needy husbands. Moreover, gender-based classifications serve to perpetuate outdated stereotypes of the respective positions of men and women in society. Statutes seeking to remedy such discrimination must be carefully drawn. If the remedial purposes may be satisfactorily achieved through the implementation of gender-neutral statutes, then an attempt by the state to discriminate on the basis of sex must be invalidated. Reversed.

EDITOR'S ANALYSIS: Note that the Court recognized the assistance of a "needy spouse" as an important state interest that may support a gender-based classification. This requires the Court to determine whether the utilization of gender is a sufficient substitute for need. Likewise, the Court has upheld gender-based classifications as a means of remedying past discrimination resulting in financial disparity between men and women in the workplace. In those cases, the Court must ascertain whether the particular area to which the statute applies is one in which women have traditionally suffered such discrimination, resulting in a difference in potential opportunities between the sexes. The Court may uphold a statute, even though it discriminates on the basis of sex, if it nonetheless is substantially related to the furtherance of these interests.

QUICKNOTES

PROXY - A person authorized to act for another.

ABSTENTION - A doctrine pursuant to which a federal court may decline to assert its authority to hear a case involving a federal question, pending resolution of an issue in the matter in state court involving a question of state law or if the matter seems more appropriately determined by a state court.

ALABAMA ALIMONY STATUTE - authorizes courts to place an obligation of alimony upon husbands but not wives.

NOTES:

STANTON v. STANTON
Divorced mother (P) v. Ex-husband (D)
421 U.S. 7 (1975).

NATURE OF CASE: Review of judgment upholding constitutional validity of a state statute.

FACT SUMMARY: Thelma Stanton (P) challenged the validity of a Utah state statute extending the period of minority for males to twenty-one years of age on the basis that it violated the state and federal constitutions.

CONCISE RULE OF LAW: A classification based on sex may only be upheld if it is reasonable and bears a fair and substantial relation to the legislature's objective in providing uniform treatment to similarly situated persons.

FACTS: Thelma (P) and Lawrence (D) Stanton were divorced in 1960. They had two children, Sherri and Rick. When Sherri reached eighteen years of age, Lawrence (D) ceased her support payments. Thelma (P) brought a motion for additional support. The court rejected the motion, and Thelma (P) appealed. Thelma (P) challenged the constitutional validity of a state statute extending the period of minority to eighteen years of age for females, and twenty-one years of age for males. The Utah Supreme Court upheld the statute. Thelma (P) appealed.

ISSUE: May a classification based on sex only be upheld if it is reasonable and bears a fair and substantial relation to the legislature's objective in providing uniform treatment to similarly situated persons?

HOLDING AND DECISION: (Blackmun, J.) Yes. A classification based on sex may only be upheld if it is reasonable and bears a fair and substantial relation to the legislature's objective in providing uniform treatment to similarly situated persons. The determinative issue is whether the difference between male and female children sustained a finding that support payments be terminated for females at eighteen years of age, and for males at twenty-one years of age. Although traditionally males may have been primarily responsible for support of the family, and females both matured and married earlier than males, such factors are not reasonably related to the objectives of the statute. Moreover, such arguments are negated by the fact that the child is deemed to have attained majority upon marriage. The state courts upon remand must determine the appropriate age of majority for children of both sexes. Reversed.

EDITOR'S ANALYSIS: The Court invokes an "intermediate scrutiny" standard of review in evaluating the constitutional validity of statutes that draw classifications on the basis of sex. This requires a court to evaluate such statutes by identifying the assumptions on which they are based and then ascertaining whether the statute furthers the legislature's proffered justifications. This inquiry necessarily entails whether the classification is actual or a result of stereotypical notions of men and women in society. Since the Equal Protection Clause requires similarly situated groups to be treated equally, this review is equally applicable to statutes that discriminate against men as well as women.

QUICKNOTES

UTAH CODE ANN. § 15-21 - extends the period of minority for males to age twenty-one and for females to age eighteen.

NOTES:

CRAIG v. BOREN
Male beer-drinker (P) v. State official (D)
429 U.S. 190 (1976).

NATURE OF CASE: Review of dismissal of action for declaratory and injunctive relief challenging the constitutional validity of a state statutory scheme.

FACT SUMMARY: Craig (P) challenged a state statutory scheme prohibiting the sale of 3.2% beer to males under twenty-one years of age and to females under eighteen years of age on the basis that it invidiously discriminated against males between the ages of eighteen and twenty-one in violation of the Equal Protection Clause of the Fourteenth Amendment.

CONCISE RULE OF LAW: A gender-based classification must be substantially related to the furtherance of an important state interest in order to be constitutionally permissible.

FACTS: Craig (P), a male between the ages of eighteen and twenty-one, commenced suit seeking declaratory and injunctive relief against the enforcement of a state statute that prohibited the sale of 3.2% beer to males under twenty-one years of age and to females under eighteen years of age. Craig (P) claimed the statute violated the Equal Protection Clause of the Fourteenth Amendment by invidiously discriminating against males between eighteen and twenty years of age. The district court upheld the statute and dismissed the action. Craig (P) appealed.

ISSUE: Must a gender-based classification be substantially related to the furtherance of an important state interest in order to be constitutionally permissible?

HOLDING AND DECISION: (Brennan, J.) Yes. A gender-based classification must be substantially related to the furtherance of an important state interest in order to be constitutionally permissible. The district court sustained the statute on the basis that it furthered the state's interest in promoting traffic safety. A variety of statistical surveys were introduced in support of that proposition demonstrating the greater propensity for males drivers between the ages of seventeen and twenty-one to be involved in accidents or to be arrested for driving under the influence. The district court held that such surveys provided a rational basis for the gender-based classification. However, even presuming the surveys were reliable, they do not sustain the constitutional validity of a gender-based classification. Courts have consistently rejected the use of more reliable statistical data supporting the use of sex as a determinative factor. In addition, the surveys offered failed to compare the difference of 3.2% beer to alcohol in general, nor did they draw a correlation between age and sex in respect to drinking and traffic-related offenses. The record failed to demonstrate that gender is an accurate substitute for the regulation of traffic safety. Reversed.

CONCURRENCE: (Stevens, J.) The determinative issue is whether the state's interest in promoting traffic safety is sufficient to sustain the constitutional validity of the statute. The record failed to demonstrate that the statute was directed toward such an objective or that it had more than a negligible effect in achieving that goal.

DISSENT: (Rehnquist, J.) The statute should be upheld under the rational basis test. The Court erred in invoking an elevated scrutiny analysis since there is no history of past discrimination against males between the ages of eighteen and twenty-one for which remedial action is necessary.

EDITOR'S ANALYSIS: The dissent sought to employ a rational basis test, requiring the state to only show that the statute bore a reasonable relationship to the furtherance of a legitimate state interest. Note that the majority held that intermediate scrutiny analysis applies as well to statutes that discriminate against males as well as to those that favor males unjustly. The Equal Protection Clause requires that equal treatment be afforded to all groups. Thus, a statute that seemingly affords women additional benefits in remedy of past discrimination, or which discriminates against men, may in actuality serve to reinforce the notions of traditional stereotypes and thus be constitutionally invalid.

QUICKNOTES

DECLARATORY RELIEF - A judgment of the court establishing the rights of the parties.

INJUNCTIVE RELIEF - A remedy imposed by the court ordering a party to cease the conduct of a specific activity.

RATIONAL BASIS TEST - A test employed by the court to determine the validity of a statute in equal protection actions, whereby the court determines whether the challenged statute is rationally related to the achievement of a legitimate state interest.

NOTES:

PERSONNEL ADMINISTRATOR OF MASSACHUSETTS v. FEENEY

State official (D) v. Prospective civil servant (P)

442 U.S. 256 (1979).

NATURE OF CASE: Review of judgment invalidating state veterans' preference statute.

FACT SUMMARY: Feeney (P) challenged the constitutional validity of a Massachusetts state statute granting veterans qualifying for state civil service positions a preference in appointment over nonveterans on the ground that the statute discriminated against women.

CONCISE RULE OF LAW: When a gender-neutral law has a disparate impact upon a group of persons that has been the victim of past discrimination, it may be unconstitutional in violation of the Equal Protection Clause.

FACTS: Feeney (P) worked for twelve years as a civil servant. During that time, she took a variety of civil service examinations on which she scored highly. Under the Massachusetts veterans' preference statute, any veteran who qualified for a civil service position must be considered for appointment before any nonveteran. As a result of the statute, Feeney (P) was placed behind less qualified veterans on the certified eligible list. Feeney (P) worked as a Senior Clerk Stenographer for the Massachusetts Civil Defense Agency for four years and was then promoted to the position of Federal Funds and Personnel Coordinator. The Agency and her job were eliminated in 1975. Feeney (P) commenced suit challenging the validity of the veterans' preference statute under the Equal Protection Clause of the Fourteenth Amendment. She contended that it discriminated against women. The district court agreed and declared the statute unconstitutional. The Personnel Administrator (D) appealed.

ISSUE: When a gender-neutral law has a disparate impact upon a group of persons that has been the victim of past discrimination, may it be unconstitutional in violation of the Equal Protection Clause?

HOLDING AND DECISION: (Stewart, J.) Yes. When a gender-neutral law has a disparate impact upon a group of persons that has been the victim of past discrimination, it may be unconstitutional in violation of the Equal Protection Clause. First the court must determine whether the classification is neutral or gender-based. If the classification is neutral, then the court must determine whether its adverse impact is the result of a discriminatory purpose. The district court concluded in this case that Massachusetts' statute furthered a legitimate state interest and that the distinction between veterans and nonveterans was not drawn with a discriminatory purpose. While females as a group do not benefit from the veteran preference statute, veteran status is not exclusively reserved to males. Moreover, substantial portion of the nonveteran population is male. This fac cannot sustain the inference that the statute served to provid males with a preference over females. Next, Feeney (P) mus demonstrate that the preference was motivated by discriminatory intent. While a statute providing a preference t veterans may be inherently gender-biased in impact, it does no evidence a gender-based discriminatory intent. Reversed.

CONCURRENCE: (Stevens, J.) The issue of whether classification is covertly gender-based should be the same a whether its adverse impact is the result of a discriminatory inten The fact that a substantial number of males were disadvantage by the impact of the statute was sufficient to warrant a conclusio that the statute was not based on a discriminatory purpose.

DISSENT: (Marshall, J.) The fact that the legislative intent is t favor one group of persons does not warrant a conclusion that did not intend to discriminate in respect to another. In order t ascertain whether a facially neutral statute was in fact motivate by a discriminatory purpose, the court must ascertain th foreseeability of a disparate impact as well as the existence o reasonably foreseeable alternatives. In order to be sustaine under an Equal Protection Clause analysis, the statute must b substantially related to the advancement of an important stat interest. Here the Administrator (D) failed to sustain that burder

EDITOR'S ANALYSIS: Note that the Equal Protection Claus does not guarantee that a statute be equitable in its impact, on that it provide equal laws to all persons. While the veteran preference statute was intentional and resulted in an advers impact on nonveterans that was necessarily foreseeable by th legislature, this does not rise to the level of discriminatory purpos required by the Equal Protection Clause. That finding requires determination that the legislature promulgated a particula regulatory scheme because of its adverse effects on a particula group.

QUICKNOTES

MASSACHUSETTS CIVIL SERVICE STATUTE - grants an absolute lifetim preference to veterans.

EEOC v. MADISON COMMUNITY UNIT SCHOOL DISTRICT NO. 12

Administrative agency (P) v. School district (D)

818 F.2d 577 (7th Cir. 1987).

NATURE OF CASE: Appeal from judgment invalidating wage discrepancies.

FACT SUMMARY: The EEOC (P) brought an action against the Madison School District (D) on the basis that it had violated the Equal Pay Act of 1963 by providing unequal pay to male and female coaches of its athletic teams.

CONCISE RULE OF LAW: The Equal Pay Act guarantees equal pay to men and women who perform equal work in employment that requires an equivalent degree of skill, effort, and responsibility and is performed under similar working conditions.

FACTS: Long, a girls' track coach in the Madison School District (D), was paid substantially less than the boys' track coach. In addition, the boys' track team had two assistant coaches, while Long only had one. Long also coached the girls' tennis team for which she received less pay than the boys' tennis team, coach, and was assistant coach of the girls' basketball team, for which she received lower pay than the boys' assistant coach, although the work of the assistant coaches were substantially equal and required the same skills and duties. Cole, the coach of the girls' volleyball, basketball and softball teams, was paid less than the coach of the boys' soccer and baseball teams. She also received less pay for her position as assistant coach of the girls' track team than the assistant coach of the boys' track team. Again, the work of the male and female coaches involved the same requisite skill and responsibilities. The EEOC (P) commenced suit against the Madison School District (D) on the basis that such discrepancies in pay violated the Equal Pay Act of 1963. The district court found in favor of the EEOC (P), and the School District (D) appealed.

ISSUE: Does the Equal Pay Act guarantee equal pay to men and women who perform equal work in employment that requires an equivalent degree of skill, effort and responsibility, and is performed under similar working conditions?

HOLDING AND DECISION: (Posner, J.) Yes. The Equal Pay Act guarantees equal pay to men and women who perform equal work in employment that requires an equivalent degree of skill, effort and responsibility, and is performed under similar working conditions. First, the court must ascertain whether the purported equal jobs constitute "equal work." While the Act requires that the positions compared have similar working conditions, it does not require that the working conditions be the same. Thus while the jobs compared must constitute equal work and require equal skill, effort and responsibilities, they need not be entirely identical. This determination is a question of fact that must be sustained unless clearly erroneous. The district court found that the coaching positions compared in the present case involved sufficiently equal work. In addition, the court held that a difference in the students' sex could not be used to maintain a disparity in pay between the coaching positions. That conclusion was erroneous in that the Act forbids an employer from using the sex of the employee to justify a pay difference, not the sex of the employee's clients. The district court's finding of equal work in this case, however, cannot be found to be clearly erroneous. After a prima facie violation has been established under the Act, the court must then consider any possible defenses. Madison (D) contended that the sex of the teams was a "factor other than sex" used in the determination of compensation. Although the Act requires that the factor other than sex refer to a factor other than the employee's sex, if the School District (D) requires the coach to be the same sex as the students and the only reason for a disparity in pay is the sex of the coach, then the Act is violated. Affirmed in part; the findings of the district court with respect to a violation of the Act in the comparison of disparate sports is vacated.

EDITOR'S ANALYSIS: Note that the Equal Pay Act does not guarantee equal compensation for men and women. Moreover, the Act does not require that wages be paid pursuant to objective factors, irrespective of the conditions of the marketplace. Thus, wage differentials paid with respect to two dissimilar jobs may be upheld under the Act, even though such disparity in pay may be the result of discrimination with respect to employment traditionally held by women compared to those traditionally held by men.

QUICKNOTES

EQUAL PAY ACT OF 1963 - provides that no employer covered by the Act shall discriminate between employees on the basis of sex.

PRIMA FACIE VIOLATION - Evidence presented by a party that is sufficient, in the absence of contradictory evidence, to support the fact or issue for which it is offered.

NOTES:

HODGSON v. ROBERT HALL CLOTHES, INC.
Secretary of Labor (P) v. Clothing store (D)
473 F.2d 589 (3d Cir.), cert. denied, 414 U.S. 866 (1973).

NATURE OF CASE: Review of the constitutional validity of an employer's payment practices.

FACT SUMMARY: The Secretary of Labor (P) challenged Robert Hall Clothes' (D) practice of paying its male salespersons a higher salary than its female salespersons.

CONCISE RULE OF LAW: Economic benefits to an employer are a sufficient justification for a wage differential under the Equal Pay Act.

FACTS: Robert Hall Clothes (D), a retail clothing store chain, sold both men's and women's clothing. The clothing in its men's department was of a higher quality and more expensive than the clothing in its women's department. As a result, the men's department consistently had a larger volume of gross sales and a higher gross profit. The store was staffed with both full-time and part-time employees. Only male employees were permitted to work in the men's department, and only female employees were permitted to work in the women's department. The employees were paid a base salary with additional incentive payments. The male employees received higher salaries than the female employees. In addition, the starting salaries and periodic increases were higher for the men, as was the amount of incentive payments. The district court ruled in favor of Robert Hall Clothes (D). The Secretary (P) appealed.

ISSUE: Are economic benefits to an employer a sufficient justification for a wage differential under the Equal Pay Act?

HOLDING AND DECISION: (Hunter, J.) Yes. Economic benefits to an employer are a sufficient justification for a wage differential under the Equal Pay Act. The Equal Pay Act expressly states that exceptions to the statute apply when male and female employees are performing equal work. Moreover, the Secretary (P) has approved commission systems based on the price of the item sold. The rationale for the approval of a wage differential paid when employees are performing equal work is based on the economic benefit to the employer. Such a wage differential is permissible regardless of whether the employee is paid commission or a base salary. In the present case, the saleswomen were paid less on the basis that the items sold in the women's department could not support a higher salary. An employer should not be made to sustain that burden. Next, the employer must demonstrate the receipt of economic benefits on which the disparity in pay was based. Robert Hall (D) sustained that burden by showing that the men's department was consistently more profitable than the women's department. Affirmed.

EDITOR'S ANALYSIS: The court also rejects the contention that an employer must demonstrate a correlation between an employee's individual performance and his or her base salary. The legislative intent behind the Equal Pay Act requires that the court not review business judgments made by employers. The imposition of a requirement that the employer correlate salary to the individual's performance would impose an undue hardship on employers and encourage systems based wholly upon commissions.

QUICKNOTES
THE EQUAL PAY ACT - provides that no employer covered by the Act shall discriminate on the basis of sex.

IN PARI MATERIA - Refers to laws or regulations pertaining to the same subject matter; under the doctrine of in pari materia, such statutes must be construed together so as to properly effectuate the legislature's intent.

TITLE VII OF THE CIVIL RIGHTS ACT OF 1964 - enacted to end employment discrimination based on race and gender.

NOTES:

CRAFT v. METROMEDIA, INC.

News anchor (P) v. Television station (D)

572 F. Supp. 868 (W.D. Mo 1983), aff'd in part, rev'd in part, 766 F.2d 1205 (8th Cir. 1985), cert. denied, 475 U.S. 1058 (1986).

NATURE OF CASE: Complaint charging gender-based discrimination in violation of Title VII of the Civil Rights Act of 1964.

FACT SUMMARY: Craft (P), a co-anchor at KMBC (D), challenged her removal from that position, charging that the station (D) had discriminated against her on the basis of sex in violation of Title VII of the Civil Rights Act of 1964.

CONCISE RULE OF LAW: An employer may enact and enforce personal appearance regulations so long as those standards are not invidiously applied.

FACTS: Craft (P) was employed as a staff announcer and co-anchor and reporter at KMBC (D). Shannon, the station's news director, and Replogle, KMBC's (D) vice president, felt that Craft's (P) on-air makeup and clothing were not appropriate. Wilford was brought to the station to assist Craft (P) in selecting her wardrobe and makeup. Subsequently, Meachem of the Media Associates conducted several focus group discussions to determine how viewers were perceiving KMBC's news program. The groups' responses to Craft's (P) appearance were extremely negative. Shannon and Replogle met with Craft (P) regarding the results of the focus groups. They agreed to work together to improve Craft's (P) perception. Media Associates then conducted a phone survey as a follow-up to its focus groups. The results of the survey showed that Craft (P) had a negative impact on viewers' perception of the station (D). Shannon and Replogle agreed to remove Craft (P) from her position as co-anchor and to reassign her to the position of reporter. Craft (P) sued, alleging that the station (D) had discriminated against her on the basis of sex.

ISSUE: May an employer enact and enforce personal appearance regulations so long as those standards are not invidiously applied?

HOLDING AND DECISION: (Stevens, J.) Yes. An employer may enact and enforce personal appearance regulations so long as those standards are not invidiously applied. Moreover, an employer may, consistent with Title VII, impose different standards in respect to male and female employees. Such regulations are related to the company's business decisions and do not constitute unfair employment practices. If an employee chooses not to comply with such regulations, he or she is subject to the company's sanctions. In the present case, KMBC's (D) appearance standards were consistent with its business objectives of providing a professional appearance to its viewers. While such standards may be discriminatory if applied invidiously, in the present case Craft (P) failed to sustain that burden.

KMBC's (D) decision to remove Craft (P) from the position of co-anchor was based on reasons other than sex.

EDITOR'S ANALYSIS: A plaintiff may assert a violation of Title VII of the Civil Rights Act of 1964 on two grounds. First, an employer's discriminatory regulations or practices may be challenged on the basis of disparate treatment. Second, under the disparate impact theory, a plaintiff may challenge a facially neutral regulation or practice on the basis that it has a disproportionate impact on women with respect to an area unrelated to the employee's job performance.

QUICKNOTES

TITLE VII OF THE CIVIL RIGHTS ACT OF 1964 - states that it shall be an unlawful employment practice for an employer to fail or refuse to hire or otherwise discriminate against any individual with respect to his employment because of such individual's race, color, religion, sex, or national origin.

NOTES:

PRICE WATERHOUSE v. HOPKINS
Employer (D) v. Partner candidate (P)
490 U.S. 228 (1989).

NATURE OF CASE: Review of ruling finding liability in gender discrimination action.

FACT SUMMARY: Hopkins (P) challenged Price Waterhouse's (D) failure to repropose her candidacy for partnership arguing that Price Waterhouse (D) had improperly discriminated on the basis of sex in violation of Title VII.

CONCISE RULE OF LAW: An employer is not liable for a violation of Title VII in making an employment decision if it demonstrates that it would have made the same decision in the absence of a discriminatory intent.

FACTS: Hopkins (P), an employee at Price Waterhouse (D), was proposed as a candidate for a partnership. At that time, seven of the 662 partners at Price Waterhouse (D) were women. Hopkins (P) was the only woman of eighty-eight candidates nominated for partnership that year. Hopkins' (P) bid for partnership was held for reconsideration the following year. The comments submitted by other partners described Hopkins (P) as aggressive, unfeminine, and deficient in interpersonal skills. An expert witness at trial testified that Price Waterhouse's (D) partnership selection process was influenced by gender-based stereotyping. The district court judge held that Price Waterhouse's (D) decision was based on legitimate factors that did not constitute a substitute for discrimination. However, the judge also ruled that some of the partners' comments were based on stereotypical notions of women that Price Waterhouse (D) made no effort to dispel. The court held Price Waterhouse (D) discriminated against Hopkins (P) in violation of Title VII on the basis that it gave effect to commentary that was based on such stereotyping. Moreover, the court found that Price Waterhouse (D) did not sustain its burden of proving by clear and convincing evidence that it would have held Hopkins' (P) candidacy in the absence of such commentary. The court of appeals affirmed. A writ of certiorari was granted by the U.S. Supreme Court.

ISSUE: Is an employer liable for a violation of Title VII in making an employment decision if it demonstrates that it would have made the same decision in the absence of a discriminatory intent?

HOLDING AND DECISION: (Brennan, J.) No. An employer is not liable for a violation of Title VII in making an employment decision if it demonstrates that it would have made the same decision in the absence of a discriminatory intent. However, the lower courts erred in holding that Price Waterhouse (D) was required to make that showing by a clear and convincing evidentiary standard.

DISSENT: (Kennedy, J.) The determinative issue in an action claiming a violation of Title VII is whether the employer's action was based on a discriminatory motive. The district court concluded that no such purpose was present and it could not conclude that Price Waterhouse's (D) board would have elected her to partnership even in the absence of gender-based stereotyping. Thus, the record demonstrated that Hopkins (P) failed to sustain her burden.

EDITOR'S ANALYSIS: The present case represents an action brought pursuant to Title VII under the disparate treatment theory. That theory is utilized to challenge an employer's regulations or decisions that are allegedly based on the employee's race, sex, religion, or national origin. In order to establish a prima facie case under the disparate treatment theory, the plaintiff must show that she was qualified for the position for which she was not hired or was subject to an adverse action and that another employee with similar qualifications was either hired or replaced her. Once a prima facie case is established, the burden of proof shifts to the employer to demonstrate a proper motive for the action or regulation.

QUICKNOTES

TITLE VII OF THE CIVIL RIGHTS ACT OF 1964 - states that it shall be an unlawful employment practice for an employer to fail or refuse to hire or otherwise discriminate against any individual with respect to his employment because of such individual's race, color, religion, sex, or national origin.

NOTES:

EZOLD v. WOLF, BLOCK, SCHORR & SOLIS-COHEN
Former senior associate (P) v. Law firm (D)
983 F.d. 509 (3d Cir. 1992), cert. denied, 510 U.S. 826 (1993).

NATURE OF CASE: Appeal from judgment granting relief for plaintiff in an employment discrimination claim under Title VII.

FACT SUMMARY: Ezold (P), a senior associate at the law firm of Wolf, Block, Schorr & Solis-Cohen (Wolf, Block) (D), contended that Wolf, Block (D) intentionally discriminated against her on the basis of sex in violation of Title VII in not admitting her to the firm's partnership.

CONCISE RULE OF LAW: When an employer relies on its subjective evaluation of the plaintiff's qualifications as the reason for denying promotion, the plaintiff can prove the reason is unworthy of credence by presenting persuasive comparative evidence that non-members of the protected class were evaluated more favorably.

FACTS: Wolf, Block (D) hired Ezold (P) as an associate on its partnership track in 1983. At that time, senior associates were evaluated annually and non-senior associates semi-annually. The partners at Wolf, Block (D) submitted written evaluations on standardized forms, listing twenty criteria of legal performance and personal characteristics. During her six-year tenure at Wolf, Block (D), Ezold (P) received both positive evaluations and evaluations questioning Ezold's (P) analytical capabilities, and her ability to meet the requirements of partnership in the firm. In addition, Ezold (P) was told to begin looking elsewhere for employment. In the 1988 partnership review, the Associates Committee voted nine to one not to recommend Ezold (P) for partnership. Ezold (P) resigned from the firm in 1989. Ezold (P) then commenced suit against Wolf (D) claiming that it intentionally discriminated against her on the basis of sex in violation of Title VII in applying stricter standards to its female associates and in not admitting her to the firm's partnership. The district court held that Wolf's (D) non-discriminatory reason for its partnership decision, i.e., that her legal analytical capabilities were insufficient, was a pretext. The district court awarded Ezold (P) backpay. Wolf, Block (D) appealed.

ISSUE: When an employer relies on its subjective evaluation of the plaintiff's qualifications as the reason for denying promotion, can the plaintiff prove the reason is unworthy of credence by presenting persuasive evidence that non-members of the protected class were evaluated more favorably?

HOLDING AND DECISION: (Hutchinson, J.) Yes. When, as in the present case, an employer utilizes a subjective, rather than objective, evaluation of an employee's qualifications for promotion, the employee can prove that the articulated reason is unworthy of credence by presenting persuasive comparative evidence that non-members of the protected class were evaluated more favorably. Pretext may not be demonstrated by showing that the employer evaluated the employee more favorably in categories not relevant to the criteria for promotion. Rather, the plaintiff must show the criteria relied upon by the employer was weak or unbelievable. Ezold (P) failed to make that showing. The district court erred in its conclusion that Wolf, Block's (D) proffered justifications were pretextual. The evidence did not demonstrate that similarly situated male associates were recommended for partnership without strong legal analytical capabilities. Such a standard is legitimate. Likewise, Ezold (P) failed to show that Wolf's (D) proffered justification was a pretext by demonstrating that a discriminatory reason was a more probable motivation for her denial of partnership. Although the partners did not grant Ezold (P) complex litigation, such decisions were a result of intellectual and not gender-based bias. Reversed and remanded.

EDITOR'S ANALYSIS: Intentional discrimination in employment cases are either "pretext" cases or "mixed-motives" cases. A pretext case requires a plaintiff to establish a prima facie case of discrimination by a preponderance of the evidence. A prima facie case is established by showing that the plaintiff was a member of a protected class, that he or she was qualified yet rejected for the particular position, and that non-members of the class received more favorable treatment. Then the burden shifts to the employer to demonstrate a legitimate, nondiscriminatory reason for the action. If there exists a genuine issue of fact, then the plaintiff loses the presumption of discrimination and he or she must prove that the employer's nondiscriminatory reason was a pretext for discrimination by a preponderance of the evidence.

QUICKNOTES
TITLE VII OF THE CIVIL RIGHTS ACT OF 1964 - states that it shall be an unlawful employment practice for an employer to fail or refuse to hire or otherwise discriminate against any individual with respect to his employment because of such individual's race, color, religion, sex, or national origin.

PRIMA FACIE CASE - An action where the plaintiff introduces sufficient evidence to submit the issue to the judge or jury for determination.

DOTHARD v. RAWLINSON
Corrections board member (D) v. Prison guard applicant (P)
433 U.S. 321 (1977).

NATURE OF CASE: Review of district court decision holding defendant liable for violation of Title VII of the Civil Rights Act of 1964 and the Equal Protection Clause.

FACT SUMMARY: Rawlinson (P) challenged the rejection of her application for the position of prison guard by the Alabama Board of Corrections (D) on the basis that it constituted impermissible gender-based discrimination in violation of Title VII and the Equal Protection Clause.

CONCISE RULE OF LAW: In order to establish a prima facie case of discrimination in respect to facially neutral employment standards, a plaintiff must demonstrate that such qualifications result in the selection of employees in a significantly discriminatory manner.

FACTS: Rawlinson (P) applied for a position as a prison guard, or "correctional counselor trainee," with the Alabama Board of Corrections (D). The Board (D) denied her application for employment on the basis that she failed to meet the minimum statutory height and weight requirements. She filed a class-action complaint in district court challenging the validity of the height and weight requirements under Title VII and the Equal Protection Clause. While this action was pending, the Board (D) enacted a regulation establishing gender requirements for correctional counselors assigned to contact positions in maximum-security facilities. Rawlinson (P) amended her complaint to challenge the validity of that regulation as well. The district court determined that the height and weight restrictions had the effect of excluding 41.13% of the female population while excluding less than 1% of the male population. The district court concluded that Rawlinson (P) had established a prima facie case of discrimination on the basis of sex.

ISSUE: In order to establish a prima facie case of discrimination in respect to facially neutral employment standards, must a plaintiff demonstrate that such qualifications result in the selection of employees in a significantly discriminatory manner?

HOLDING AND DECISION: (Stewart, J.) Yes. In order to establish a prima facie case of discrimination in respect to facially neutral employment standards, a plaintiff must demonstrate that such qualifications result in the selection of employees in a significantly discriminatory manner. Then the burden shifts to the employer to demonstrate that the requirement bears a direct relationship to the nature of the employment. If the employer sustains that burden, then the plaintiff may demonstrate that the employer's objective could be achieved through other nondiscriminatory means. Here the Board (D) contended that a

showing of disparate impact required Rawlinson (P) to introduce an analysis based on the characteristics of the actual applicants for the position of correctional counselor and not on national statistics. However, Title VII does not require that the plaintiff introduce evidence regarding the characteristics of the actual applicants. Moreover, such evidence may not accurately reflect the potential applicant pool as many applicants may be discouraged from applying due to the height and weight requirements. Thus, the district court did not err in concluding that Rawlinson (P) established a prima facie case of disparate impact. The Board (D) also failed to demonstrate a correlation between the requirements and the required amount of strength necessary for the position. In establishing that a discriminatory standard is a bona fide occupational qualification (BFOQ), an employer must adopt a means of determining a basis for measuring the strength of the individual applicants. The Board (D) failed to provide such evidence. In contrast, the regulation specifically excluding women from maximum security contact positions is discriminatory on its face. The Board (D) contended that such regulation fell within the bona fide occupational qualification defense to Title VII. That defense permits an employer to overtly discriminate on the basis of sex when such discrimination is reasonably necessary for the operation of the business. Here the district court erred, however, in concluding that the regulation did not fall within the BFOQ exception. Affirmed in part, reversed in part, and remanded.

CONCURRENCE AND DISSENT: (Marshall, J.) The purpose of Title VII is to permit women to decide for themselves whether or not to enter a particular field of employment.

EDITOR'S ANALYSIS: When a plaintiff establishes a prima facie case of disparate treatment, the only defense available to the employer is to demonstrate that the qualification fits within the bona fide occupational qualification exception. This so-called BFOQ exception is a narrow exception to the general rule that an employer may not discriminate on the basis of sex in its employment practices. In order to avail itself of the defense, an employer must demonstrate that the absence of the requirement would result in the "undermining" of the nature of the enterprise.

QUICKNOTES

TITLE VII OF THE CIVIL RIGHTS ACT OF 1964 - states that it shall be an unlawful employment practice for an employer to fail or refuse to hire or otherwise discriminate against any individual with respect to his employment because of such individual's race, color, religion, sex, or national origin.

PRIMA FACIE CASE - An action where the plaintiff introduces sufficient evidence to submit the issue to the judge or jury for determination.

BONA FIDE OCCUPATIONAL QUALIFICATION - A statutory exception to the prohibition on discrimination in employment if the individual's sex, religion or national origin is a necessary qualification for the operation of the business.

WILSON v. SOUTHWEST AIRLINES CO.
Male job applicant (P) v. Airline
517 F. Supp. 292 (N.D. Tex. 1981).

NATURE OF CASE: Class action suit claiming an employer's hiring practices violated Title VII of the Civil Rights Act of 1964.

FACT SUMMARY: Wilson (P) commenced a class action suit on behalf of himself and 100 other male job applicants, claiming that Southwest Airlines (D) violated Title VII through its policy of hiring only females for the positions of flight attendant and ticket agent.

CONCISE RULE OF LAW: An employer may consider sex as a bona fide occupational qualification only when it is reasonably necessary to the continued operation of the business.

FACTS: Southwest Airlines (D) employed an advertising agency in 1971 to develop a marketing strategy. The agency developed Southwest's (D) "Love" campaign, which was embodied in an attractive female in order to appeal to Southwest's (D) primarily male business passengers. Consistent with that campaign, Southwest (D) had a policy of employing only females in the high customer contact position of ticket agent and flight attendant. Wilson (P) commenced a class action suit on behalf of himself and 100 other male job applicants, claiming that Southwest (D) violated Title VII by refusing to hire men for the job categories of ticket agent and flight attendant. Southwest (D) contended that such practice was justified and exempted from Title VII's ban on sex discrimination as a bona fide occupational qualification (BFOQ) because its attractive flight attendants were the largest single component of its success and its overall "love image" had enhanced its ability to attract passengers.

ISSUE: May an employer consider sex as a bona fide occupational qualification only when it is reasonably necessary to the continued operation of the business?

HOLDING AND DECISION: (Higginbotham, J.) Yes. An employer may consider sex as a bona fide occupational qualification only when it is reasonably necessary to the continued operation of the business. The BFOQ exception does not justify the refusal to hire a particular person based on the preferences of its clientele, except if necessary for authenticity, such as in the case of an actor or actress. This circuit has adopted a two-part test for determining whether a job qualification constitutes a BFOQ. First the court must determine whether the particular position requires that the employee be of a particular sex. If the answer is yes, then the court must determine whether that requirement is reasonably necessary to the "essence" of the enterprise. The employer must show that the qualification is so essential to the business that its operation would be "undermined" if it did not hire members of a particular sex. In order for sex to be recognized as a BFOQ in a job category requiring a number of skills, the sex-based abilities must predominate in order to satisfy the "essence" requirement. In the present case, the requirement that an employee be female is not essential to the performance of the positions of flight attendant and ticket agent, whose duties are predominantly mechanical. The primary function of Southwest (D) is the safe transport of its customers. That function would not be undermined by the hiring of males for the positions of flight attendant and ticket agent. Judgment for Wilson (P).

EDITOR'S ANALYSIS: Once a plaintiff establishes a prima facie case of discrimination based on the theory that the particular job requirement has a disparate impact on one gender, the burden shifts to the employer to demonstrate that the hiring criterion is justified as a business necessity. Some jurisdictions construe the business necessity defense as broader than the BFOQ defense. Courts have generally limited their finding that customer preference may be considered to situations in which sex or sex appeal is the primary service provided by the enterprise. Similarly, courts have suggested that nationality may be a legitimate requirement when necessary to maintain the authenticity of the enterprise, such as an ethnic restaurant.

QUICKNOTES

TITLE VII OF THE CIVIL RIGHTS ACT OF 1964 - states that it shall be an unlawful employment practice for an employer to fail or refuse to hire or otherwise discriminate against any individual with respect to his employment because of such individual's race, color, religion, sex, or national origin.

BONA FIDE OCCUPATIONAL QUALIFICATION - A statutory exception to the prohibition on discrimination in employment if the individual's sex, religion or national origin is a necessary qualification for the operation of the business.

PRIMA FACIE CASE - An action where the plaintiff introduces sufficient evidence to submit the issue to the judge or jury for determination.

NOTES:

UAW v. JOHNSON CONTROLS, INC.

Female employees (P) v. Battery manufacturer (D)

499 U.S. 187 (1991).

NATURE OF CASE: Review of court of appeals decision affirming grant of summary judgment to an employer in a class action suit for violation of Title VII of the Civil Rights Act of 1964.

FACT SUMMARY: Employees (P) of Johnson Controls (D) brought a class action suit contending that its fetal-protection policy, excluding women from positions of employment involving lead exposure, constituted impermissible discrimination on the basis of sex in violation of Title VII.

CONCISE RULE OF LAW: An employer's implementation of a gender-based, fetal-protection policy constitutes sex discrimination in violation of Title VII, unless the employer can show that sex is a "bona fide occupational qualification."

FACTS: Johnson Controls (D), a battery manufacturer, did not employ women in battery-manufacturing positions prior to the enactment of Title VII. The manufacture of batteries utilizes lead as a primary ingredient, which has been demonstrated to lead to health risks, including harm to a fetus of a pregnant employee. Following the enactment of Title VII, Johnson Controls (D) announced that it would discourage women from entering such positions and require them to sign a statement that they had been advised of the pertinent health risks. Five years later, Johnson Controls (D) instituted a policy totally excluding women from such positions, since eight of its female employees became pregnant while incurring blood lead levels above the critical level as determined by the Occupational Health and Safety Administration (OSHA). The policy expressly excluded women "capable of bearing children." UAW (P) commenced a class action suit, claiming that such practice constituted unlawful discrimination on the basis of sex in violation of Title VII. The district court granted summary judgment for Johnson Controls (D) on the basis that UAW (P) had failed to demonstrate a satisfactory alternative policy. Furthermore, the court held that the business necessity defense did not require Johnson Controls (D) to conduct a bona fide occupational qualification's (BFOQ) analysis. The court of appeals affirmed. The Supreme Court granted UAW's (P) petition for certiorari.

ISSUE: Does an employer's implementation of a gender-based, fetal-protection policy constitute sex discrimination in violation of Title VII, unless the employer can show that sex is a "bona fide occupational qualification"?

HOLDING AND DECISION: (Blackmun, J.) Yes. An employer's implementation of a gender-based, fetal-protection policy constitutes sex discrimination in violation of Title VII, unless the employer can show that sex is a "bona fide occupational

qualification." The employment policy at issue here expressly allows men, and not women, employees of Johnson Controls (D) to choose whether to accept employment that may endanger their reproductive abilities, thereby creating a classification based on sex. Although male employees are subject to similar health risks by exposure to lead, the policy only requires its female employees to show evidence that they are incapable of having children. In its 1982 statement, Johnson Controls (D) specifically excluded women who are capable of bearing children from positions involving lead exposure. That policy demonstrated discrimination on the basis of sex in violation of Title VII. Thus, Johnson Control's (D) fetal-protection policy is unconstitutional unless it can demonstrate that gender is a "bona fide occupational qualification" (BFOQ). Johnson Controls (D) contended that its fetal-protection policy fell within the BFOQ's safety exception. This Court has held that when the safety concerns of third parties relate to the essence of an employer's business, then a job qualification may constitute a BFOQ. In the present case, however, the safety concerns of the female employees' unborn fetuses are not third parties whose safety is necessary to the enterprise of battery manufacturing. Furthermore, the Pregnancy Discrimination Act (PDA) requires women who are pregnant or potentially pregnant to be treated the same as other employees with similar abilities to work. The decision of whether to become pregnant and to continue working during her pregnancy is reserved to the individual woman. Thus, an employer may not discriminate against a female employee based on her potential to become pregnant, unless the employer can demonstrate that such potential will interfere with the performance of the duties of her position that are essential to the particular business. Johnson Controls (D) failed to sustain that burden. Reversed and remanded.

CONCURRENCE: (White, J.) The PDA was enacted not to restrict the scope of the BFOQ defense, but rather to clarify the definitions under Title VII. The majority erroneously discounts the possibility of tort liability by employers for prenatal injuries sustained by the unborn children of their employees.

CONCURRENCE: (Scalia, J.) The different treatment of women on the basis of pregnancy constitutes discrimination on the basis of sex, regardless of whether men were similarly affected.

EDITOR'S ANALYSIS: Title VII prohibits classifications in the terms and conditions of employment on the basis of gender. Furthermore, the PDA provides that discrimination on the basis of sex also includes discrimination related to pregnancy, childbirth, or other related reasons. In order to fall within the BFOQ exception, the qualification at issue must either pertain to the "essence" or "mission" of the employer's business.

BOARD OF DIRECTORS OF ROTARY INTERNATIONAL v. ROTARY CLUB OF DUARTE

International organization (D) v. Local club (P)

481 U.S. 537 (1987).

NATURE OF CASE: Review of action alleging violations of Unruh Civil Rights Act.

FACT SUMMARY: The Rotary Club of Duarte (P) challenged the constitutional validity of Rotary International's (D) termination of its membership for the admission of three women members on the basis that such action violated the Unruh Civil Rights Act.

CONCISE RULE OF LAW: An individual's freedom to enter into and carry on intimate or private relationships is a fundamental liberty interest under the First Amendment.

FACTS: Rotary International (D) is a nonprofit organization of professional men. Individual members belong to a local Rotary Club that in turn is a member of International (D). Individual membership is based on a classification system. Individual members must work in leadership positions within their organization. Each individual Rotary Club may enact its own rules and procedures for admitting members, subject to the limitation that membership is only available to men. The Rotary Club of Duarte (P) admitted three women. International (D) revoked the Duarte Club's (P) charter and terminated its membership in International (D). The Duarte Club (P) commenced a civil action charging International (D) with violation of the Unruh Civil Rights Act. That Act provided that all Californians were entitled to full services in all business establishments.

ISSUE: Is an individual's freedom to enter into and carry on intimate or private relationships a fundamental liberty interest under the First Amendment?

HOLDING AND DECISION: (Powell, J.) Yes. An individual's freedom to enter into and carry on intimate or private relationships is a fundamental liberty interest under the First Amendment. Courts have afforded protection to freedom of association under the First Amendment on two grounds. The First Amendment prohibits government interference with a person's freedom to enter into intimate or private relationships. In addition, an individual's freedom to associate in order to participate in protected speech or religious activities is also protected. The court must consider several factors such as the size, purpose, selectivity, and exclusivity of the particular relationship in determining whether to afford it constitutional protection. Here the record demonstrated that membership in a Rotary Club is not the type of intimate or private relationship in which the Constitution affords a liberty interest. The size and transiency of the individual clubs do not constitute a intimate relationship for First Amendment purposes. Moreover, the purpose of the clubs is to provide an inclusive membership. In addition, although Rotary Club membership is not open to the general public, members are encouraged to invite business associates and other visitors to the meetings. In light of its policy to keep its "windows and doors open to the whole world," the application of the Unruh Act to local Rotary Clubs does not violate their members' liberty interest in freedom of association. This Court has also protected an individual's right to associate with other individuals who share the members' particular objectives. In the present case, however, the record did not demonstrate that admission of female members would impede the ability of the Rotary Club members to achieve their organizational objectives. While the Rotary Clubs perform a variety of service activities within the community, such purpose is not abandoned by the admission of female members. Moreover, such a requirement only enhances the organization's purpose in representing a cross-section of the community in its membership. In addition, any small infringement on the Rotary Club members' rights of association is justified by the state's compelling interest in eliminating discrimination on the basis of sex.

EDITOR'S ANALYSIS: Note that federal statutes do not apply to private organizations such as Rotary International (D). Thus, a challenge to a gender-based membership requirement must be brought pursuant to state law. While state civil rights statutes vary according to jurisdiction, plaintiffs typically commence suit challenging that the particular practice violates the First Amendment right to freedom of association.

QUICKNOTES

UNRUH CIVIL RIGHTS ACT - California law providing that all persons within the jurisdiction of the state are free and equal and entitled to full and equal accomodations, advantages, and services in all business establishments.

NOTES:

ISBISTER v. BOYS' CLUB OF SANTA CRUZ, INC.
Prospective member (P) v.
Private nonprofit recreational club (D)
Cal. Sup. Ct., 707 P.2d. 212 (1985).

NATURE OF CASE: Appeal from judgment enjoining organization's membership regulations under the Unruh Civil Rights Act.

FACT SUMMARY: Several girls (P) challenged their denial of membership to the Boys' Club of Santa Cruz (D) on the basis that such membership restrictions were in violation of the Unruh Civil Rights Act.

CONCISE RULE OF LAW: The Unruh Civil Rights Act prohibits arbitrary discrimination on the basis of sex by a business establishment.

FACTS: The Boy's Club (D), a private nonprofit organization, owned and operated a recreational facility. Use of the Club's (D) facilities were only open to members. Membership was available to all male children between the ages of eight and eighteen. Several girls (P) were denied membership to the Club (D) due to its practice of restricting membership solely to males. The girls (P) sought injunctive and declaratory relief and charged the Club (D) with violations of the Unruh Civil Rights Act. The district court issued the injunction, and the Boys' Club (D) appealed.

ISSUE: Does the Unruh Civil Rights Act prohibit arbitrary discrimination on the basis of sex by a business establishment?

HOLDING AND DECISION: (Grodin, J.) Yes. The Unruh Civil Rights Act prohibits arbitrary discrimination on the basis of sex by a business establishment. The Boys' Club (D) constitutes a business establishment falling within the purviews of the Act. Thus, its practice of restricting membership to males only constitutes a violation of state statute. The Boys' Club (D) asserted that such membership restrictions furthered the legitimate interest in deterring delinquency amongst male children. While delinquency also affects a substantial number of girls, the Boys' Club (D) provided no evidence that the admission of girls would diminish its efficiency in achieving that goal. In addition, the Boys' Club (D) contended that the admission of girls may cause it to lose sources of revenue. This argument failed to recognize that the admission of girls may in fact provide new sources of revenue for the Club (D). Affirmed.

DISSENT: (Mosk, J.) The classification of the Boys' Club (D) as a "business establishment" is erroneous and presents severe implications for children's organizations throughout the state.

DISSENT: (Kaus, J.) The majority excluded the expansion of its opinion to organizations that operate facilities not open to the general public or that show a compelling need for segregation based on sex. In order to constitute a facility not open to the general public, the facility must offer services to a broad segment of the population except for a particular group that has traditionally been the victim of past discrimination. The record failed to support that finding. Moreover, the Boys' Club (D) demonstrated a compelling need for segregation on the basis of sex. The majority erroneously presumed that the intent of establishing the Boys' Club (D) was for the exclusion of girls and not the provision of a service to boys.

EDITOR'S ANALYSIS: Note that federal legislation does not apply to challenges to gender-based exclusions from private clubs or associations, which must be brought pursuant to state law. A subsequent challenge to the exclusion of girls from the Boy Scouts under the Unruh Act was rejected. In that case, the court held that the Boy Scouts did not constitute a "business establishment" and thus did not fall within the purview of the Act.

QUICKNOTES
UNRUH CIVIL RIGHTS ACT - California law providing that all persons within the jurisdiction of the state are free and equal and entitled to full and equal accomodations, advantages, and services in all business establishments.

IPSE DIXIT - A statement by an individual whose authority for the proposition is the fact that he himself has said it.

NOTES:

CHAPTER 3
SUBSTANTIVE EQUALITY

QUICK REFERENCE RULES OF LAW

1. **Sex-Specific Public Benefits to Remedy Past Societal Discrimination.** A statue affording different treatment on the basis of sex may be upheld if it is based on a distinction that has a fair and substantial relation to the legislation's objectives. (Kahn v. Shevin)

2. **"Affirmative Action" in Hiring.** An affirmative action plan designed to remedy the effects of past discrimination in the workplace is valid under Title VII. (Johnson v. Transportation Agency)

3. **"Comparable Worth:" Challenging the Economic Structure.** In order to sustain a claim of employment discrimination based on disparate wages between predominantly male and female job positions, a plaintiff must show that the employer was motivated by a discriminatory purpose. (American Nurses' Association v. Illinois)

4. **Eliminating the Disadvantage of Women's Differences: Pregnancy.** A state statute requiring employers to provide leave and reinstatement benefits to employees who are disabled on the basis of pregnancy is valid and consistent with federal law. (California Federal Savings & Loan Association v. Guerra)

5. **Eliminating the Disadvantage of Women's Differences: Pregnancy.** The PDA requires an employer to treat pregnant employees the same as it would treat similarly affected, nonpregnant employees. (Troupe v. May Department Stores Co.)

6. **Eliminating the Disadvantages of Women's Differences: Work and Family.** Homemaking is not employment for the purposes of determining work-release privileges. (State v. Bachmann)

7. **Recognizing Sex-Linked Average Differences: Fringe Benefit Plans, Insurance, and Other Actuarially-Based Systems.** An employment practice violates Title VII if the record shows that the person was treated in a manner that would have been different but for the person's sex. (City of Los Angeles, Department of Water & Power v. Manhart)

8. **Recognizing Sex-Linked Average Differences: Eligibility for School Athletic Teams.** The maintenance of a separate school-sponsored athletic team, and separate events in that sport, for girls is constitutionally valid and consistent with the requirements of due process. (Petrie v. Illinois High School Association)

9. **Recognizing Sex-Linked Average Differences: Eligibility for School Athletic Teams.** Education is not a fundamental right subject to strict scrutiny analysis. (O'Connor v. Board of Education of School District 23)

10. **Recognizing Sex-Linked Average Differences: Sex-Segregated Schools.** Discrimination based on sex is unconstitutional unless it is substantially related to important government objectives. (United States v. Virginia)

11. **Recognizing Sex-Linked Average Differences: Equality in School Athletic Programs.** Title IX requires that an institution allocate its athletics resources and provide opportunities for both sexes in a non-discriminatory manner. (Cohen v. Brown University)

12. **The Gender Gap in Divorce Reform.** In order to obtain the remedy of a constructive trust, the proponent must show that he made a transfer of the property to the trustee in reliance on a promise that such property would be held for the proponent's benefit, and that the trustee would be unjustly enriched if permitted to retain the property. (Saff v. Saff)

13. **The Gender Gap in Divorce Reform.** If a spouse detrimentally relies on the other for monetary support, rehabilitative maintenance should be awarded for a term reasonably sufficient to receive job training. (Michael v. Michael)

14. **The Gender Gap in Divorce Reform.** Under the "equitable" approach to rehabilitative support, the period of payment of spousal support must address the burdens of the divorce and make up for the opportunities and development a disadvantaged spouse lost while assuming her economic role in the marriage. (Riehl v. Riehl)

15. **Feminism: The Maternal Presumption Revisited.** The tender years doctrine is a relevant factor in deciding the primary residence of a young child. (DeCamp v. Hein)

16. **Feminism: The Maternal Presumption Revisited.** Comparative income or economic advantage is not a permissible basis for a custody award. (Burchard v. Garay)

17. **Feminism: The Maternal Presumption Revisited.** The primary caretaker is the natural or adoptive parent who, until the commencement of divorce proceedings, has been primarily responsible for the care and nurturing of the child. (Patricia Ann S. v. James Daniel S.)

18. **Feminism: The Maternal Presumption Revisited.** Decisions regarding child custody are governed by the "best interests of the child" standard. (In re Marriage of Elser)

19. **Feminism: The Maternal Presumption Revisited.** In cases where the custodial parent wants to relocate the children, that party need not show that such move is necessary. Rather, the court will consider the presumptive right of the parent to change the residence of the children so long as the move would not be prejudicial to their rights or welfare. (Burgess v. Burgess

20. **Unmarried Parents.** A state statute distinguishing between the rights of unmarried mothers and unmarried fathers is unconstitutional in violation of the Equal Protection Clause, unless it is demonstrated that such classification is substantially related to an important state interest. (Caban v. Mohammed)

21. **Unmarried Parents.** A federal statute governing citizenship requirements for children born out of wedlock to a U.S. citizen abroad is constitutional, despite the fact that it treats men and women differently, because it serves an important governmental interest. (Nguyen v. Immigration and Naturalization Service)

KAHN v. SHEVIN
Widower (P) v. State official (D)
416 U.S. 351 (1974).

NATURE OF CASE: Review of the constitutional validity of a state statute providing a property tax exemption to widows.

FACT SUMMARY: Kahn (P), a widower, challenged the denial of his application for a property tax exemption specifically for widows on the basis that the statute providing for the exemption was unconstitutional in violation of the Equal Protection Clause.

CONCISE RULE OF LAW: A statue affording different treatment on the basis of sex may be upheld if it is based on a distinction that has a fair and substantial relation to the legislation's objectives.

FACTS: A Florida law provided widows with a $500 annual property tax exemption. Kahn (P), a widower residing in Florida, applied for the exemption. Kahn's (P) application was denied by the Dade County Tax Assessor's Office on the basis that the statute only provided the exemption to widows. The circuit court held the statute unconstitutional in violation of the Equal Protection Clause of the Fourteenth Amendment. The Florida Supreme Court reversed. The Supreme Court granted certiorari.

ISSUE: May a statue affording different treatment on the basis of sex be upheld if it is based on a distinction that has a fair and substantial relation to the legislation's objectives?

HOLDING AND DECISION: (Douglas, J.) Yes. A statue affording different treatment on the basis of sex may be upheld if it is based on a distinction that has a fair and substantial relation to the legislation's objectives. The record demonstrated that women in Florida (D) were only able to obtain the lowest paying forms of employment. Statistics showed that the average salary for a working woman was only 57.9% of the average salary for males. Moreover, a male may continue in his occupation following his spouse's death, whereas a woman is more likely to be forced into the job market. Here the statute does not afford a benefit to women only on the basis of administrative convenience. Rather, the statute at issue furthers the State's (D) objective in mitigating the financial impact of the death of a spouse on the party who suffers a disproportionate loss. Affirmed.

DISSENT: (Brennan, J.) A statute classifying persons solely on the basis of sex for the receipt of public benefits is subject to strict scrutiny analysis as it is based wholly on immutable characteristics. While the statute serves the compelling state interests of remedying the economic impact of past discrimination towards women, the State (D) failed to demonstrate that it could attain such an objective through a more narrowly tailored statute or by less restrictive means. Moreover, the State (D) failed to demonstrate how the $500 property tax exemption furthered the objective of the legislation.

DISSENT: (White, J.) The gender-based classification at issue constitutes invidious discrimination in violation of the Equal Protection Clause. The State (D) has failed to provide an adequate justification for that classification.

EDITOR'S ANALYSIS: The present action is one of the few instances in which the Supreme Court sustained a statute conditioning the receipt of public benefits on the basis of sex for the purpose of remedying past discrimination. Such statutes are based on "substantive equality," which judges the statute's results or effects in its treatment of women and men. Such statutes attempt to remedy the effects of past discrimination by providing opportunities to women in employment fields traditionally dominated by men, or by implementing equivalent payment scales for both sexes.

NOTES:

JOHNSON v. TRANSPORTATION AGENCY
Male employee (P) v. State employer (D)
480 U.S. 616 (1987).

NATURE OF CASE: Review of appellate court judgment upholding affirmative action plan.

FACT SUMMARY: Johnson (P) challenged the County Transportation Agency's (D) denial of his promotion to the position of road dispatcher on the basis that it constituted discrimination on the basis of sex in violation of Title VII.

CONCISE RULE OF LAW: An affirmative action plan designed to remedy the effects of past discrimination in the workplace is valid under Title VII.

FACTS: In 1978, the Santa Clara County Transit District Board of Supervisors adopted an affirmative action plan for the County Transportation Agency (D). The plan provided that the Agency (D) was permitted to consider sex as a factor in making promotions to positions that had traditionally been segregated. The Agency (D) stated that its intent was to annually improve in its hiring, training and promotion of women and minorities to positions in which they had been traditionally underrepresented. The Agency's (D) objective was to achieve a work force composed of a proportion of women and minorities equal to that existing in the labor force. In 1979, the Agency (D) announced a vacancy in the promotional position of road dispatcher. The Agency's (D) goal was that 36% of that classification would eventually be occupied by women. Twelve County employees applied for the position, including Joyce, a female applicant and Johnson (P), a male applicant. Nine of the applicants were deemed qualified for the position and were interviewed by the board. Johnson (P) tied for second with a score of 75. Joyce placed fourth with a score of 73. Johnson (P) filed a complaint with the EEOC claiming that he was denied promotion on the basis of gender in violation of Title VII. The district court held in favor of Johnson (P). The court of appeals reversed. Johnson (P) appealed.

ISSUE: Is an affirmative action plan designed to remedy the effects of past discrimination in the workplace valid under Title VII?

HOLDING AND DECISION: (Brennan, J.) Yes. An affirmative action plan designed to remedy the effects of past discrimination in the workplace is valid under Title VII. The plaintiff bears the burden of demonstrating that the employer's practice violated Title VII. Here the first issue is whether the consideration of the employees' gender was justified by the presence of a "manifest imbalance" of males and females in traditionally segregated job categories. The determination of whether such an imbalance exists is made by comparing the percentage of females represented in the job category with the percentage of females in the labor force of the particular area. If the position requires a special skill, the comparison must be with those persons in the labor force possessing that skill. Here women were substantially underrepresented in the Skill Craft category, since 100% of the 238 positions in that category were filled by men. Next it must be determined whether the plan violated the rights of male employees or created a prohibition on their advancement. The plan at issue merely required gender to be one of the factors taken into consideration in the overall assessment. Moreover, Johnson (P) was not absolutely entitled to the position of road dispatcher, and his denial did not displace such an expectation. Last, the plan was designed in order to achieve a balanced work force, not in order to maintain one. Affirmed.

CONCURRENCE: (Stevens, J.) The Civil Rights Act of 1964 does not mandate an employer to grant preferential treatment to employees on the basis of race or gender; however, employers may adopt voluntary programs to benefit the members of protected groups. Such programs should not be restricted to the remedy of past discrimination in violation of Title VII, but should also take into account future considerations.

CONCURRENCE: (O'Connor, J.) The evaluation of the legitimacy of an affirmative action plan under Title VII is the equivalent of an Equal Protection Clause analysis. Affirmative action programs are only permissible as a remedy to alleviate the effects of discrimination.

DISSENT: (Scalia, J.) The majority's opinion transforms Title VII from a prohibition on the consideration of race or sex in employment decisions to a guarantee that race or sex will be a factor in such decisions.

EDITOR'S ANALYSIS: Note that the Supreme Court has subsequently invalidated race-based programs implemented by employers in order to achieve an employee pool reflective of the labor force. The Court has struck down such government set-aside programs under a strict scrutiny analysis. Furthermore, the Court had previously struck down a race-based affirmative action admissions plan implemented by the University of California on the basis that it improperly used race as a criteria in determining admission. The Court stated that while race may not constitute a determinative factor, it may be one factor in the total evaluation.

QUICKNOTES
TITLE VII OF THE CIVIL RIGHTS ACT OF 1964 - states that it shall be an unlawful employment practice for an employer to fail or refuse to hire or otherwise discriminate against any individual with respect to his employment because of such individual's race, color, religion, sex, or national origin.

AMERICAN NURSES' ASSOCIATION v. ILLINOIS

State employees (P) v. State of Illinois (D)

783 F.2d. 716 (7th Cir. 1986).

NATURE OF CASE: Appeal from dismissal of a class action complaint charging the state with discrimination in employment on the basis of sex.

FACT SUMMARY: Two associations (P) of nurses and individual employees (P) filed a class action complaint against the State of Illinois (D), claiming that the State's (D) employment practices were discriminatory in that it paid higher wages to predominantly male positions not justified by any relative worth.

CONCISE RULE OF LAW: In order to sustain a claim of employment discrimination based on disparate wages between predominantly male and female job positions, a plaintiff must show that the employer was motivated by a discriminatory purpose.

FACTS: Two associations (P) of nurses and twenty-one individuals (P) who worked for the State of Illinois (D) in the positions of nurses and typists commenced suit on behalf of all state employees in those job classifications, claiming that the State (D) paid workers in predominantly male positions higher wages than workers in predominantly female positions. The district court dismissed the complaint on the basis that the State's (P) failure to pay its employees in accordance with comparable worth did not violate Title VII. The associations (P) appealed.

ISSUE: In order to sustain a claim of employment discrimination based on disparate wages between predominantly male and female job positions, must a plaintiff show that the employer was motivated by a discriminatory purpose?

HOLDING AND DECISION: (Posner, J.) Yes. In order to sustain a claim of employment discrimination based on disparate wages between predominantly male and female job positions, a plaintiff must show that the employer was motivated by a discriminatory purpose. The associations (P) contended that a failure to attain comparable worth may be evidence of unlawful discrimination and distinct from the mere payment of market-based wages. Other circuits have held that an employer's failure to conduct comparable worth studies are alone insufficient to infer a discriminatory motive, but that a decision to phase in over the period of ten years a wage system based on the results of a comparable worth study constituted discrimination on the basis of sex. Thus, when an employer pays market wages that are disproportionate in respect to predominantly male and female positions, such payment does not constitute a violation of Title VII, even if the employer is aware that such payment departs from comparable worth and results in a disadvantage to female employees. The determinative issue is whether the State (D)

decided not to raise the wages of certain positions on the basis that they were predominantly held by women. The inference of a violation of Title VII from the mere fact that an employer conducted a comparable worth study would discourage such studies. Likewise, the associations' (P) equal protection claim fails as well. The Supreme Court has held that the Equal Protection Clause requires a showing of intentional discrimination. When the state promulgates a law or practice with a lawful purpose, the demonstration of disparate impact is not sufficient to sustain a finding of a discriminatory purpose. That finding requires a demonstration that the employer chose a particular practice for the purpose of disfavoring a particular group. Thus, the State's (D) payment of market wages is alone insufficient to demonstrate discriminatory purpose, even if the State (D) was aware that such payments would result in lower wages for predominantly female positions. Discriminatory purpose requires a demonstration that the State (D) failed to remedy the practice on the basis that it intended to cause or maintain the discrepancy. Moreover, if the State (D) intentionally segregated jobs on the basis of gender, then a violation of Title VII may be sustained. The associations (P) contend that the State (D) knew or should have known of the traditional disparity in treatment between males and females which was shown in part by the comparable worth study. That study, however, merely showed that the State (D) provided disparate wages consistent with the prevailing market wages. The fact that the State (D) did not depart from market wages in order to satisfy notions of comparable worth is not sufficient to sustain a violation of Title VII. The associations (P) failed to demonstrate that the State (D) was motivated by the theory that men are entitled to higher wages than women despite their performance of equal work. Reversed and remanded.

EDITOR'S ANALYSIS: "Comparable worth" refers to a movement to equalize the discrepancy in wages between traditionally male and female positions in the marketplace. The doctrine of comparable worth has both historical and psychological bases. Proponents of the comparable worth doctrine contend that society has historically encouraged women to enter into certain positions and intentionally kept the wages for those positions at a depressed rate. Moreover, they argue that the relative worth of positions typically held by men and women may be calculated even if those positions involve unequal work.

CALIFORNIA FEDERAL SAVINGS & LOAN ASSOCIATION
v. GUERRA
Federally chartered savings and loan assoc. (P) v.
State official (D)
479 U.S. 272 (1987).

NATURE OF CASE: Review of court of appeals' decision upholding the validity of a state statute.

FACT SUMMARY: California Federal Savings & Loan (Cal Fed) (P) sought declaratory and injunctive relief from the operation of a state statute requiring employers to provide leave and reinstatement benefits to employees who were disabled on the basis of pregnancy, claiming that the statute was preempted by Title VII of the Civil Rights Act of 1978, as amended by the Pregnancy Discrimination Act of 1978 (PDA).

CONCISE RULE OF LAW: A state statute requiring employers to provide leave and reinstatement benefits to employees who are disabled on the basis of pregnancy is valid and consistent with federal law.

FACTS: Cal Fed (P), a federally chartered savings and loan association, had a facially neutral leave policy permitting its employees to take unpaid leaves of absence following their first three months of employment. While Cal Fed (P) attempted to provide employees taking leave with a similar position upon their return, it expressly reserved the right to terminate that employee's employment if such position was no longer available. Garland, a receptionist for Cal Fed (P), took a pregnancy disability leave. When Garland sought to return to her position, she was informed that it was no longer available. Garland filed a complaint with the Department of Fair Employment and Housing (D). The Department (D) charged Cal Fed (P) with violations of § 12945(b) of the Fair Employment and Housing Act (FEHA). That section requires employers to provide pregnant employees with unpaid disability leave of up to four months. The statute has also been interpreted to require the employer to return the employee to her previous position, unless it is no longer available due to business necessity. In that case, the employer is required to make a reasonable, good-faith effort to provide the employee with substantially similar employment. While Title VII prohibits employment discrimination on the basis of sex, the Supreme Court has held that such discrimination did not include discrimination on the basis of pregnancy. In response to that decision, Congress enacted the Pregnancy Discrimination Act of 1978 (PDA) in order to clarify that discrimination on the basis of sex includes discrimination on the basis of pregnancy. Prior to the administrative hearing, Cal Fed (P) commenced suit in district court seeking a declaration that § 12945(b)(2) of FEHA was inconsistent with, and preempted by, Title VII and seeking an injunction against the enforcement of the statute. The district court granted summary judgment for Cal Fed (P). The court of appeals reversed. Cal Fed (P) petitioned for certiorari, and the Supreme Court granted review.

ISSUE: Is a state statute requiring employers to provide leave and reinstatement benefits to employees who are disabled on the basis of pregnancy valid and consistent with federal law?

HOLDING AND DECISION: (Marshall, J.) Yes. A state statute requiring employers to provide leave and reinstatement benefits to employees who are disabled on the basis of pregnancy is valid and consistent with federal law. The court of appeals held that the legislative intent behind the PDA was to provide a minimum, and not a maximum, requirement for pregnancy disability benefits. In enacting the PDA, Congress concluded that there was pervasive evidence of discrimination on the basis of pregnancy in the provision of disability and health insurance programs. Moreover, Congress recognized the existence of state laws prohibiting discrimination on the basis of pregnancy and suggested that such statutes would continue to be operative under the PDA. The state at issue here and Title VII, as amended by the PDA, both were enacted in order to ensure women an equal opportunity to compete in the workplace. Furthermore, the statute allows both men and women to exercise their right to have families. Section 12945(b)(2) is narrowly tailored to apply only to the period of actual physical disability on account of pregnancy. In addition, the statute is not based on archaic or stereotypical ideas of pregnancy and the abilities of pregnant employees. Last, the state statute is not incompatible with federal law. Section 12945(b)(2) does not require employers to treat pregnancy employees better than other disabled employees; rather, it establishes a minimum level of benefits that employers are required to provide to such employees. Affirmed.

DISSENT: (White, J.) Section 12945(b)(2) is in conflict with the PDA and is thus preempted. While the PDA requires that all pregnant employees be treated the same for employment purposes as similarly situated nonpregnant employees, § 12945(b)(2) requires an employer to provide disability leave for pregnant employees even when it does not provide similar benefits for employees with other disabilities. The legislative history reflects an intent on the part of Congress to provide equal treatment in enacting the PDA.

Continued on next page.

EDITOR'S ANALYSIS: The PDA was enacted in response to a Supreme Court holding that discrimination in respect to pregnancy did not constitute discrimination on the basis of sex. Prior to that holding, the Court upheld the exclusion of pregnancy from a list of disability benefits under an Equal Protection Clause analysis. The Court stated that pregnancy is not a sex-based classification per se. Moreover, in the absence of a demonstration that such classifications are motivated by a discriminatory intent, such statutes excluding pregnancy from the list of compensable disabilities are subject only to a rational basis review. Regardless of that result, the Court has subsequently held certain regulations discriminating against pregnant women as constitutionally impermissible.

QUICKNOTES

PREGNANCY DISCRIMINATION ACT OF 1978 - mandates that pregnant employees shall be treated the same for all employment-related purposes as nonpregnant employees similarly situated with respect to their ability or inability to work.

CAL. GOVT. CODE ANN. § 12945 (b) (2) - requires employers to provide female employees an unpaid pregnancy disability leave of up to four months and a qualified right to reinstatement.

NOTES:

TROUPE v. MAY DEPARTMENT STORES CO.
Terminated saleswoman (P) v. Employer (D)
20 F.3d 734 (7th Cir. 1994).

NATURE OF CASE: Review of the validity of an employee's termination under the Pregnancy Discrimination Act of 1978 (PDA).

FACT SUMMARY: Troupe (P), an employee of Lord & Taylor Department Store, challenged the termination of her employment as in violation of the PDA, contending that she was fired because her supervisor did not think she would return to work following her maternity leave.

CONCISE RULE OF LAW: The PDA requires an employer to treat pregnant employees the same as it would treat similarly affected, nonpregnant employees.

FACTS: Troupe (P), an employee of Lord & Taylor Department Store, experienced unusually severe morning sickness during her first trimester of pregnancy. She requested to be returned to part-time status, working only between the hours of 12:00 p.m. and 5:00 p.m. Troupe (P) continued to experience morning sickness at work, causing her to be excessively tardy and to leave work early on a consistent basis. She received an oral warning by her immediate supervisor. The following day, Troupe (P) was late again. She was then issued a written warning. Troupe (P) continued to be tardy and was placed on a sixty-day probation. During that period she was late on eleven occasions, and was subsequently fired. The firing took place the day before she was scheduled to commence her maternity leave. Troupe (P) testified that she was terminated because her supervisor did not believe that she would return to work following her leave.

ISSUE: Does the PDA require an employer to treat pregnant employees the same as it would treat similarly affected, nonpregnant employees?

HOLDING AND DECISION: (Posner, J.) Yes. The PDA requires an employer to treat pregnant employees the same as it would treat similarly affected, nonpregnant employees. The PDA does not mandate that employers either provide maternity leave or facilitate the return of pregnant women to work. The PDA simply requires that employers provide equal treatment to pregnant and nonpregnant employees. Troupe (P) failed to demonstrate that she would not have been fired but for her pregnancy. Moreover, she did not show that nonpregnant employees were treated more favorably than pregnant employees. Action dismissed.

EDITOR'S ANALYSIS: Note that had Troupe (P) introduced evidence to demonstrate that comparable absences by nonpregnant employees were not punished by termination, the outcome in the case may have been different. The court required only that pregnant women be afforded equal treatment as similarly situated, nonpregnant employees under the PDA. Furthermore, the PDA does not require that an employer provide a pregnant employee with "special" treatment.

QUICKNOTES

PREGNANCY DISCRIMINATION ACT OF 1978 - mandates that pregnant employees shall be treated the same for all employment-related purposes as nonpregnant employees similarly situated with respect to their ability or inability to work.

NOTES:

STATE v. BACHMANN

State of Minnesota (P) v. Housewife convicted of forgery (D)

521 N.W.2d 886 (Minn. Ct. App. 1994).

NOTES:

NATURE OF CASE: Appeal of denial of post conviction relief.

FACT SUMMARY: Bachmann (D), a housewife, was convicted of forgery and burglary and then denied post-conviction relief on the grounds that she was not eligible for work-release privileges. She filed this appeal.

CONCISE RULE OF LAW: Homemaking is not employment for the purposes of determining work-release privileges.

FACTS: Bachmann (D) was a housewife who was convicted of forgery and burglary. She had requested work-release privileges during her 90-day sentence so that she could care for her four children during the week while her husband worked. Her husband had agreed to compensate her at a rate of $1.50 an hour for her labor. The District Court found that Bachmann (D) was ineligible for work-release privileges and she filed this appeal.

ISSUE: Does housekeeping constitute employment for the purposes of determining work-release privileges?

HOLDING AND DECISION: (Schumacher, J.) No. While it is true that housekeeping has economic value, it does not constitute employment. First, Bachmann (D) is obligated to care for her children regardless of whether she receives compensation for providing that service. Second, the income Bachmann (D) receives for performing these duties is marital property. Her husband has a property interest in the money he gives her. Therefore, their wage agreement is not like a typical employment agreement because neither party loses or gains wages. The property belongs to both parties at all times. The economic exchange between husband and wife is purely illusory. Accordingly, this Court affirms the ruling of the District Court.

EDITOR'S ANALYSIS: While the Court acknowledges that housework has economic value, it refuses to acknowledge that a homemaker is deserving of compensation. The Court goes into a lengthy tangent about the sacredness of the home and how the home is meant to be a sanctuary from industry where the power of affection prevails. Essentially, the Court determines that love is not only the motivation for the homemaker's labor but that it should be her only form of compensation.

CITY OF LOS ANGELES, DEPARTMENT OF WATER & POWER v. MANHART

City department (D) v. Female employee (P)

435 U.S. 702 (1978).

NATURE OF CASE: Review of judgment ordering refund of excess contributions to pension plan made in violation of Title VII.

FACT SUMMARY: Employees (P) brought a challenge to the City of Los Angeles Department of Water & Power's (D) practice of requiring its female employees to make greater pension fund contributions than its male employees.

CONCISE RULE OF LAW: An employment practice violates Title VII if the record shows that the person was treated in a manner that would have been different but for the person's sex.

FACTS: The Department (D) administered retirement, disability, and death-benefit programs for its employees. Each employee was entitled to a monthly payment comprising a fraction of his or her salary multiplied by the years the employee worked. The monthly benefits for males and females of equal position and salary were equivalent. The Department (D) determined that the average life expectancy for one of its female employees exceeded that of its males employees. Since the cost to the Department (D) was greater for those employees, the women were required to make monthly contributions to the pension fund that were 14.84% higher than the contributions required of male employees. This resulted in a lower net salary to the female employees. Subsequently, California legislature enacted a law barring municipal agencies from requiring females to make such higher contributions. The Department (D) changed its pension scheme. The district court held the contribution differential in the former plan was in violation of Title VII and required a refund of such contributions. The court of appeal affirmed. The Supreme Court granted review.

ISSUE: Does an employment practice violate Title VII if the record shows the person was treated in a manner that would have been different but for the person's sex?

HOLDING AND DECISION: (Stevens, J.) Yes. An employment practice violates Title VII if the record shows the person was treated in a manner that would have been different but for the person's sex. Title VII prohibits the unlawful discrimination against any individual in respect to the conditions of employment based on that person's race, color, religion, sex, or national origin. Individuals may not be discriminated against based on general characteristics of the group to which they belong, even if such generalizations are true. In the present case, the Department (D) made the true generalization that women live longer than men in organizing its pension fund scheme. The

Department (D) failed to realize, however, that there is no guarantee that the individual women employed by the Department (D) will in fact live longer than the Department's (D) male employees. Furthermore, the female employees received smaller paychecks during their lives on the basis of sex and are not assured to receive an offsetting advantage upon retirement. The Department (D) contended that permitting women to pay the same contributions into the pension fund was unfair since it will require the male employees to subsidize the women's retirement benefits. The question of fairness, however, should be left to the legislature. Congress has determined that classifications on the basis of sex are prohibited. The intent behind Title VII is that individuals, and not the classes to which they belong, be treated fairly. The classification of employees based on the group to which they belong serve to perpetuate traditional notions regarding those groups, and precludes individual consideration. Affirmed.

CONCURRENCE AND DISSENT: (Burger, C.J.) The life insurance, annuity, and pension plan industry has always relied upon actuarial tables in assessing its pension programs. The Equal Pay Act expressly exempts differentials in pay based upon factors other than sex. In the present case, that factor is longevity. Moreover, it would be impossible to formulate a pension plan to the particular circumstances of each individual employee. Thus, the application of valid statistical data should be permissible.

EDITOR'S ANALYSIS: Enacted in 1963, The Equal Pay Act requires employers to compensate men and women on an equal basis for equal work, subject to four exceptions. One such exception permits a pay differential that is based on any "factor other than sex." In the present case, the Department (D) argued that the different contributions required of its male and female employees were based on the alternative factor of longevity. The Court found, however, that the record was devoid of any such intent on the part of the Department (D).

QUICKNOTES

TITLE VII OF THE CIVIL RIGHTS ACT OF 1964 - states that it shall be an unlawful employment practice for an employer to fail or refuse to hire or otherwise discriminate against any individual with respect to his employment because of such individual's race, color, religion, sex, or national origin.

PETRIE v. ILLINOIS HIGH SCHOOL ASSOCIATION
Male student (P) v. Voluntary association of state schools (D)
Ill. Ct. App., 394 N.E.2d 855 (1979).

NATURE OF CASE: Review of judgment upholding validity of a school restriction on participation.

FACT SUMMARY: Petrie (P), a sixteen-year-old male high school student, challenged a school rule restricting interscholastic competition on the only school-sponsored volleyball team to girls.

CONCISE RULE OF LAW: The maintenance of a separate school-sponsored athletic team, and separate events in that sport, for girls is constitutionally valid and consistent with the requirements of due process.

FACTS: Petrie (P), a sixteen-year old male high school student, reported and practiced with the Champaign Central High School volleyball team. School officials informed Petrie (P) that he was barred from competition with other schools pursuant to a rule restricting membership on the only school-sponsored volleyball team to girls. Petrie (P) sued the Illinois High School Association (D), which ran the volleyball tournament for girls only. The district court ruled against Petrie (P), and he appealed.

ISSUE: Is the maintenance of a separate school-sponsored athletic team, and separate events in that sport, for girls constitutionally valid and consistent with the requirements of due process?

HOLDING AND DECISION: (Green, J.) Yes. The maintenance of a separate school-sponsored athletic team, and separate events in that sport, for girls is constitutionally valid and consistent with the requirements of due process. The maintenance of a separate team advances the important government objectives of furthering athletic opportunities for girls. The rule at issue excluded boys from participation on the basis that such participation would have the effect of excluding girls. The record demonstrated that girls are at a substantial disadvantage to boys in playing volleyball. Sports has a long-standing tradition of classifying persons based on objectively measured physical characteristics. Petrie (P) contended that teams should be classified based on objective physical characteristics not related to sex. Such a system, however, would be difficult to construct. Furthermore, the classification of public high school teams on the basis of sex is predicated on the innate physical differences between the sexes, not on stereotypical or paternalistic notions of the sexes. While such classifications are necessarily both under and overbroad, it is the only feasible means of furthering the state's interest in advancing interscholastic athletics for girls. The maintenance of a separate volleyball team and tournaments for girls furthers such state interest. Affirmed.

DISSENT: (Craven, J.) While the majority seeks to further a legitimate state objective, it does so through impermissible means. The Due Process Clause prohibits classifications based on general presumptions regarding the sexes, when individually those presumptions are rebuttable.

EDITOR'S ANALYSIS: Note that the court held that boys were prohibited from competing on the girls' athletic team although the school did not provide a comparable boys' team. Courts have held that girls, however, are entitled to compete for boys' teams in the absence of comparable teams for girls. Furthermore, courts have held that girls are entitled to an opportunity to compete for both contact and non-contact boys' teams, when no girls' team is provided.

NOTES:

O'CONNOR v. BOARD OF EDUCATION OF SCHOOL DISTRICT 23

Female student (P) v. School board (D)

645 F.2d 578 (7th Cir. 1981), cert. denied, 454 U.S. 1084 (1981).

NATURE OF CASE: Review of district court decision granting a preliminary injunction restraining a board of education from refusing to allow a girl student to try out for a boys' athletics team.

FACT SUMMARY: O'Connor (P) sought an injunction restraining the Board of Education (D) from refusing to permit her to try out for the boys' sixth grade basketball team.

CONCISE RULE OF LAW: Education is not a fundamental right subject to strict scrutiny analysis.

FACTS: O'Connor (P), an eleven-year-old sixth grade female student, sought permission to try out for the boys' interscholastic basketball team. The Board of Education (D) rejected her application, but invited O'Connor (P) to participate on the girls' team. The district court granted a preliminary injunction against the Board (D). The district court applied a strict scrutiny analysis and concluded that the Board (D) had violated O'Connor's (P) fundamental rights to develop and to an education and that the Board (D) failed to demonstrate that the school's athletics program was the least restrictive alternative. The Board (D) appealed. The enforcement of the preliminary injunction was stayed pending the appeal.

ISSUE: Is education a fundamental right subject to strict scrutiny analysis?

HOLDING AND DECISION: (Bauer, J.) No. Education is not a fundamental right subject to strict scrutiny analysis. The determinative question in the present case was whether O'Connor (P) could show a reasonable likelihood that the separate team approach was not substantially related to the state's objective in maximizing children's participation in athletics. O'Connor (P) failed to sustain that burden. The program treats the two teams identically in respect to funding, facilities and other criteria. Courts have upheld schools' maintenance of separate teams for both sexes. The Board (D) demonstrated such programs furthered its objective in increasing girl students' participation in athletics. Reversed and remanded.

EDITOR'S ANALYSIS: Formal equality requires that similar groups or individuals receive similar treatment based on their individual characteristics and not stereotypical notions of the class to which they belong. In cases where two separate athletic teams are provided to both boys and girls, formal equality may be provided in respect to the group as a whole, but not to its individual members. It may not be possible to achieve formal equality on an individual basis, since an individual may be restricted based on general characteristics of his or her gender.

QUICKNOTES

STRICT SCRUTINY - Method by which courts determine the constitutionality of a law, when a law affects a fundamental right. Under the test, the legislature must have a compelling interest to enact law and measures prescribed by the law must be the least restrictive means possible to accomplish goal.

PRELIMINARY INJUNCTION - An order issued by the court at the commencement of an action, requiring a party to refrain from conducting a specified activity that is the subject of the controversy, until the matter is determined.

NOTES:

UNITED STATES v. VIRGINIA

Federal government (P) v. Military college supporter (D)

518 U.S. 515 (1996).

NATURE OF CASE: Appeal in an action challenging the constitutionality of public college admission policy.

FACT SUMMARY: Virginia (D) created the Virginia Women's Institute for Leadership (VWIL) to avoid equal protection problems with Virginia Military Institute's (VMI) (D) male-only admission policy.

CONCISE RULE OF LAW: Discrimination based on sex is unconstitutional unless it is substantially related to important government objectives.

FACTS: VMI (D), a public university, had a policy of only admitting male students. VMI (D) sought to provide a military education to its students through physical rigor and adversative methods. In 1990, a female high school student filed a complaint challenging this admission policy, and the United States (P) sued the Commonwealth of Virginia (D) and VMI (D) alleging that the male-only admission policy violated the Equal Protection Clause of the Fourteenth Amendment. The Fourth Circuit ruled against VMI (D). In response, Virginia (D) proposed a parallel program for women, the VWIL. Although VWIL purportedly would have fulfilled the same mission as VMI (D), its program offered significantly different programs and had far fewer resources. The district court ruled that the creation of VWIL satisfied the requirements of the Equal Protection Clause, and the court of appeals affirmed.

ISSUE: Is discrimination based on sex unconstitutional unless it is substantially related to important government objectives?

HOLDING AND DECISION: (Ginsburg, J.) Yes. Discrimination based on sex is unconstitutional unless it is substantially related to important government objectives. In 1971, the Supreme Court held for the first time that sex-based classifications may deny equal protection. Since then, the Court has consistently found that government laws and policies which deny women equal opportunity are unconstitutional. Although the Court has not found that sex-based classifications demand strict scrutiny, as do race classifications, the Court has held that a state must show that the sex discrimination serves an important government objective and that the means employed are substantially related to the achievement of those objectives. VMI (D) claimed that single-sex education provides important educational benefits by providing diversity in approaches. However, the history of Virginia's (D) public school policy demonstrates that the male-only admission policy was not actually created in furtherance of a state policy of diversity. Additionally, VMI (D) failed to show that its methods and goals are inherently unsuitable for women. Some women may want to pursue the type of education offered by VMI (D). The proposed VWIL is clearly inadequate and unequal in its ability to offer women a similar experience. Therefore, Virginia's (D) equal protection violation is not remedied by the proposed creation of VWIL. Reversed.

CONCURRENCE: (Rehnquist, C.J.) Virginia's (D) options are not as limited as the majority claims. If Virginia (D) had made a genuine effort to devote comparable resources to a facility for women, it might have avoided an equal protection violation.

DISSENT: (Scalia, J.) Women are not a discrete and insular minority deserving of equal protection consideration. Furthermore, even if "intermediate scrutiny" were the correct way to analyze sex-based classifications, the majority failed to properly apply this test in the current case.

EDITOR'S ANALYSIS: Justice Scalia's dissent is accurate in pointing out the majority's failure to expressly apply the intermediate scrutiny test. However, his argument that sex-based discrimination deserves only rational basis review based on the political power of women is unpersuasive. After all, women still comprise a very small minority in the state and federal legislatures.

QUICKNOTES

STRICT SCRUTINY - Method by which courts determine the constitutionality of a law, when a law affects a fundamental right. Under the test, the legislature must have a compelling interest to enact law and measures prescribed by the law must be the least restrictive means possible to accomplish goal.

INTERMEDIATE SCRUTINY - A standard of reviewing the propriety of classifications pertaining to gender or legitimacy, under the Equal Protection Clause of the United States Constitution, which requires a court to ascertain whether the classification furthers an important state interest and is substantially related to the attainment of that interest.

RATIONAL BASIS REVIEW - A test employed by the court to determine the validity of a statute in equal protection actions, whereby the court determines whether the challenged statute is rationally related to the achievement of a legitimate state interest.

COHEN v. BROWN UNIVERSITY

Female student (P) v. University (D)

101 F.3d 155 (1st Cir. 1996), cert. denied, 520 U.S. 1186 (1997).

NATURE OF CASE: Appeal from order in class action suit ordering reinstatement of teams demoted in violation of Title IX of the Education Amendments of 1972.

FACT SUMMARY: Female students (P) commenced a class action suit, claiming that Brown University (D) discriminated on the basis of sex in violation of Title IX by demoting two of its women's teams from university-funded to donor-funded varsity status.

CONCISE RULE OF LAW: Title IX requires that an institution allocate its athletics resources and provide opportunities for both sexes in a non-discriminatory manner.

FACTS: Brown University (D), a Division I National Collegiate Athletic Association institution, demoted its women's gymnastics and volleyball teams from university-funded varsity status to donor-funded varsity status in 1991. Brown (D) similarly demoted its men's water polo and golf teams to donor-funded status. The teams lost not only their university funding, but many privileges associated with university-funded status. Cohen (P) commenced suit on behalf of the class comprising all present, future, and potential Brown female students who participated, sought to participate, or were deterred from participation in university-funded intercollegiate athletics, charging Brown (D), its president (D), and its athletics director (D) with discrimination on the basis of sex in violation of Title IX. The district court granted Cohen's (P) motion for a preliminary injunction reinstating the women's gymnastics and volleyball teams to university-funded status and prohibiting the further change in status of any women's intercollegiate athletics team pending the outcome of the litigation. The court of appeals affirmed and remanded for a trial on the merits. On remand, the district court concluded that Brown (D) had violated Title IX and ordered Brown (D) to submit a comprehensive plan for compliance. The district court rejected the plan submitted by Brown and ordered the women's teams to be reinstated at university-funded varsity status. Brown (D) appealed.

ISSUE: Does Title IX require that an institution allocate its athletics resources and provide opportunities for both sexes in a non-discriminatory manner?

HOLDING AND DECISION: (Bownes, J.) Yes. Title IX requires that an institution allocate its athletics resources and provide opportunities for both sexes in a non-discriminatory manner. Title IX prohibits any person from exclusion in, the denial of benefits from, or the subjection to discrimination on the basis of sex under any educational program that receives federal aid. In this case, Brown (D) contended that the district court improperly applied a three-part test, requiring the court to determine: (1) whether opportunities for intercollegiate athletic participation were provided for both males and females in proportion to their percentage in the student body; (2) whether the institution can demonstrate a policy of program expansion in areas in which one sex has been underrepresented; and (3) if the members of one sex are underrepresented and the institution cannot show a policy of program expansion, whether it can show the interests and abilities of the members of that sex have been considered and accommodated by the current policy. Brown (D) contended that the test mandates preferential treatment for females, rendering Title IX an "affirmative action statute," and that the test itself is in violation of Title IX and unconstitutional. Title IX is an anti-discrimination statute that allows the implementation of affirmative action programs as a result of the inference that gender-based discrimination exists based on a demonstration of statistical disparity. The Supreme Court has applied an intermediate scrutiny analysis to all cases involving equal protection challenges to gender-based classifications. Under this standard, the state must show that the classification serves important governmental objectives and the means employed are substantially related to the achievement of those objectives. Applying that test, the district court's remedial order passes constitutional muster. The state's interests in preventing the use of federal funds to support discriminatory practices and in protecting the public against such practices are important government interests. Moreover, the district courts' remedy requiring an institution to eliminate, add, or elevate certain athletics teams is substantially related to the attainment of those objectives. Affirmed in part, reversed in part, and remanded.

DISSENT: (Torruella, J.) All gender-based state action should be subject to the same standard of review, regardless of whether it is classified as benign or remedial. The majority erroneously applied a more lenient standard of intermediate scrutiny in the present case. The proponent of the gender-based government classification denying opportunities to members of one sex should be required to demonstrate an "exceedingly persuasive justification" for the action.

EDITOR'S ANALYSIS: Brown (D) also contended that the disparity in athletics opportunities for males and females was the result of a lower level of interest in athletics on the part of female students, not the result of discrimination. The court stated, however, that a lower rate of participation in women's athletics is properly attributable to their traditionally lower level of opportunity for participation in athletics. Thus, even if it could be demonstrated that statistically women had less interest in athletics, such evidence alone did not provide a justification for providing female students with fewer opportunities to participate in intercollegiate athletics.

SAFF v. SAFF
Wife (P) v. Husband (D)
N.Y. Sup. Ct., App. Div., 402 N.Y.S.2d 690 (1978), appeal dismissed,
415 N.Y.S.2d 829 (1979).

NATURE OF CASE: Appeal from denial of request for alimony payments and the imposition of a constructive trust.

FACT SUMMARY: Clara (P) sought to receive alimony payments and requested the court to impose a constructive trust on one-half the separate property of her husband.

CONCISE RULE OF LAW: In order to obtain the remedy of a constructive trust, the proponent must show that he made a transfer of the property to the trustee in reliance on a promise that such property would be held for the proponent's benefit, and that the trustee would be unjustly enriched if permitted to retain the property.

FACTS: When Leonard (D) and Clara Saff (P) were married, Clara (P) was employed as a maid and Leonard (D) was unemployed. They gradually accumulated funds that they held in their joint names. Leonard (D) subsequently entered into a partnership and founded Jamestown Fabricated Steel. Each partner invested $2,000. Leonard (D) loaned the other partner, Dahl, $1,000 so that he could purchase his interest. The money for the partnership interests was paid from the Saffs' joint funds. Subsequently the company was incorporated and its stock divided between Leonard (D) and Dahl. At the time of the divorce, the corporation had a net worth of approximately $500,000 and grossed $590,000 annually. Clara (P) did not hold a legal interest in the company or the stock. Clara (P) obtained a divorce from her husband on grounds of abandonment. She appealed from the lower court's judgment denying her alimony and rejecting her claim that a constructive trust be placed on one-half Leonard's (D) separate property.

ISSUE: In order to obtain the remedy of a constructive trust, must the proponent show that he made a transfer of the property to the trustee in reliance on a promise that such property would be held for the proponent's benefit, and that the trustee would be unjustly enriched if permitted to retain the property?

HOLDING AND DECISION: (Simons, J.) Yes. In order to obtain the remedy of a constructive trust, the proponent must show that he made a transfer of the property to the trustee in reliance on a promise that such property would be held for the proponent's benefit, and that the trustee would be unjustly enriched if permitted to retain the property. Here, Clara (P) must demonstrate that Leonard (D) made an express or implied promise causing her to transfer property to him, that a confidential relationship exists between them, and that Leonard (D) was unjustly enriched by the transfer. The marriage did constitute a confidential relationship, and there was a transfer of property by Clara (P) to Leonard (D). However, there was no express or implied promise that Leonard (D) held one-half of the stock in his corporation for Clara's (P) benefit. While Clara (P) contended that Leonard (D) made representations to her that she was entitled to half of his assets, such casual statements did not constitute a grant of one-half his interest in his corporate stock. Neither did Leonard (D) impliedly promise that he held such stock as a trustee for Clara's (P) benefit. The existence of the marital relationship alone does not give rise to an implied promise sufficient to sustain the enforcement of a constructive trust. Moreover, the court must distinguish between promises that are made in respect to the marital relationship from those made in respect to a business relationship. The remedy of a constructive trust may not be imposed in order to adjust disparity between spouses or as a punitive measure. In this case, the existence of the marital relationship warranted a conclusion that the services rendered by Clara (P) on behalf of the corporation were part of the normal incidents of marriage for which she received ample consideration. Such services may not be interpreted as earning her an interest in the corporation. Although Leonard (D) transferred jointly held funds to acquire the company, such transfer was not induced by either the confidential marital relationship or in reliance on either an express or implied promise. Finally, Leonard (D) was not unjustly enriched. Clara (P) received the benefits of the corporation for over thirty years. Affirmed.

DISSENT: (Cardamone, J.) The facts and circumstances of the Saffs' marriage warrant a conclusion that Clara (P) should be permitted to impose a constructive trust on one-half the corporate stock. From the commencement of their marriage, the Saffs jointly held all their property. Clara (P) not only transferred her interest in the jointly held marital property, but contributed her time and labor to the advancement of the corporation.

EDITOR'S ANALYSIS: A "constructive trust" is an equitable remedy imposed by the court in order to prevent the unjust enrichment of the legal holder of the alleged trust res. A constructive trust is a legal fiction by which the legal holder is deemed to have held the property in trust for the benefit of the wronged party. The court will impose a constructive trust if one party has been wrongfully deprived of some right to property through mistake, fraud, or breach of duty.

QUICKNOTES
CONSTRUCTIVE TRUST - A trust that arises by operation of law whereby the court imposes a trust upon property lawfully held by one party for the benefit of another, as a result of some wrongdoing by the party in possession so as to avoid unjust enrichment.

MICHAEL v. MICHAEL
Husband (P) v. Wife (D)
791 S.W.2d 772 (Mo. Ct. App. 1990).

NATURE OF CASE: Appeal of divorce judgment.

FACT SUMMARY: Wife (D) was awarded the majority of the marital property and Husband (P) received no maintenance and $500 attorney's fees. Husband (P) appeals the divorce judgment.

CONCISE RULE OF LAW: If a spouse detrimentally relies on the other for monetary support, rehabilitative maintenance should be awarded for a term reasonably sufficient to receive job training.

FACTS: Husband (P) was laid off from his job as a journalist and he and Wife (D) agreed that he would stay home and write fiction. In the meantime, Wife (D) earned a substantial amount of money and provided for Husband (P). For a period of about ten years, Husband (P) was not working as a journalist and remained home to tend to household duties. When Husband (P) and Wife (D) divorced, the Court granted wife 75.5% of the marital estate and Husband (P) received only 21.5%. Additionally, Husband (P) did not receive maintenance of any kind, but was awarded attorney's fees. Husband (P) appealed the divorce judgment.

ISSUE: Is a spouse who is unemployed and tends to household duties while relying on the other spouse for support entitled to rehabilitative maintenance upon the dissolution of the marriage?

HOLDING AND DECISION: (Pudlowski, J.) Yes. We view marriage as a shared partnership. Throughout the course of this marriage, Husband (P) became economically dependent on his wife. At the time of the dissolution of this marriage, Husband (P) had not been employed in his field for about fifteen years. During that time, Wife (D) had developed her career and had been the sole financial support of the parties. The lower court found that Husband (P) had not contributed as much to the household as Wife (D). However, while his performance of many household chores was lax, Husband (P) did drive Wife (D) to and from work and prepare dinner every night. Therefore, while we do not believe that Husband (P) is entitled to an equal share of the marital property, we find that the lower court abused its discretion in granting Husband (P) such a small portion of the property. Additionally, we find that because Husband (P) detrimentally relied on Wife (D) for financial support and did not work in his field for so many years, he is entitled to rehabilitative maintenance so that he can complete the proper training to return to work in his field.

DISSENT: (Crandall, J.) I would affirm the decree of dissolution because I think it is clear that Husband (P) has not been unable to provide for himself but that he is unwilling to do so. He did not contribute to the partnership of marriage but, rather, acted as a hindrance to Wife's (D) financial and professional progress.

EDITOR'S ANALYSIS: How would the Court's decision be different if the gender roles in this relationship were reversed? Traditionally, it is women who have sought compensation for housework and for assistance in developing work skills after the dissolution of the marriage. The husband in this case performed minimal household duties, except for preparing dinner, which he admittedly enjoyed and found stimulating. Presumably, the wife ended up performing the household tasks as well as acting as the primary breadwinner. However, the Court chose to compensate the husband for his performance of one household duty that women have been traditionally expected to perform.

NOTES:

RIEHL v. RIEHL
Wife (P) v. Husband (D)
595 N.W.2d 10 (N.D. 1999).

NATURE OF CASE: Appeal of spousal support order.

FACT SUMMARY: Deborah Riehl (P) and Andrew Riehl (D) were married for 24 years. Deborah (P) appeals from a district court judgment granting the divorce, dividing the marital property, placing the children in Deborah's (P) custody, and ordering Andrew (D) to pay rehabilitative support only for the period of time it takes Deborah (P) to be rehabilitated.

CONCISE RULE OF LAW: Under the "equitable" approach to rehabilitative support, the period of payment of spousal support must address the burdens of the divorce and make up for the opportunities and development a disadvantaged spouse lost while assuming her economic role in the marriage.

FACTS: Deborah (P) and Andrew (D) were married for 24 years. During that time, Deborah (P) put off developing a career in order to care for their children and act as a homemaker. After years in her role as a homemaker, Deborah decided to pursue a career in nursing. Deborah's (P) starting salary after completing a nursing program would equal about half of Andrew's (D) salary. The trial court awarded Deborah (P) five years of rehabilitative support, or support for the amount of time it would take for her to finish her nursing program and become minimally self-sufficient. Deborah (P) appeals the trial court's decision.

ISSUE: Is five years of rehabilitative support sufficient to make up for the opportunities and development a spouse lost while assuming the role of homemaker in a marriage for 24 years?

HOLDING AND DECISION: (Maring, J.) No. There are two approaches to awarding rehabilitative spousal support. This Court has rejected the "minimalist doctrine" which has the objective of restoring the disadvantaged spouse to minimal self-sufficiency. Instead, we have adopted the "equitable" approach, which attempts to provide education or training that will enable the disadvantaged spouse to receive "appropriate" self-support while improving her employment skills. In determining what constitutes "appropriate" support, the Court will consider the duration of the marriage, the parties' respective earning capacities, and the value of the marital property. In the case at bar, the parties stipulated to an equal division of marital property. The property division, therefore, did not address the parties' disparate earning capacities. Awarding Deborah (P) five years of rehabilitative support would perhaps have been sufficient under the minimalist doctrine. However, under the equitable doctrine, the support order must mitigate the disadvantage caused by the economic role assumed during the marriage. Deborah's (P) earning capacity was dramatically reduced by her role as a homemaker for 24 years.

Additionally, after five years, should she complete her training, she will begin in the field of nursing with an entry-level salary that will equal about half of what Andrew (D) makes. Accordingly, we find that an order for five years of rehabilitative support is insufficient and clearly erroneous.

EDITOR'S ANALYSIS: This case illustrates the difficulties courts have encountered in attempting to determine how to compensate spouses who have been disadvantaged by playing the role of homemaker within a marriage. Courts have begun to recognize the economic consequences of such a role, but they continue to differ as to how to address the resulting financial inequities upon dissolution of the marriage.

NOTES:

DECAMP v. HEIN

Parties not identified

Fla. Dist. Ct. App., 541 So. 2d. 708 (1989).

NATURE OF CASE: Review of trial court's decision in a child custody suit.

FACT SUMMARY: Appeal from a lower court decision determining the proper residence of two baby girls, ages one and three.

CONCISE RULE OF LAW: The tender years doctrine is a relevant factor in deciding the primary residence of a young child.

FACTS: (Facts not stated.)

ISSUE: Is the tender years doctrine a relevant factor in deciding the primary residence of a young child?

HOLDING AND DECISION: (Letts, J.) Yes. The tender years doctrine is a relevant factor in deciding the primary residence of a young child. This requires that an infant who is being nursed by its mother necessarily be maintained in the mother's custody. While the record does not demonstrate whether the one-year old in this case was being nursed by the mother, the facts require that the one-year old and her three-year old sister be maintained in their mother's custody. The court has recognized a psychologist's testimony that from the ages of one through four the mother is the essential person in a child's life. Thus, the children in the present case should be in their mother's custody, unless the judge found her unfit.

EDITOR'S ANALYSIS: Traditionally, fathers possessed an almost absolute right to custody of the children following the marriage. The theory supporting that doctrine was that the father had a duty to support and maintain his children; thus, he in turn was entitled to benefit from the children's services. The "tender years doctrine" marked the first move towards the granting of maternal custody; however, it only afforded such custody to mothers for the early years of childhood after which custody reverted to the father.

QUICKNOTES

TENDER YEARS DOCTRINE - children under the age of four should reside with their mother.

NOTES:

BURCHARD v. GARAY
Mother (P) v. Father (D)

Cal. Sup. Ct., 42 Cal. 3d 531, 229 Cal. Rptr. 800. 724 P.2d 486 (1986).

NATURE OF CASE: Appeal from trial court order awarding custody of a child to the father.

FACT SUMMARY: The trial court awarded custody of Burchard's two and one-half-year old son, to his father, Garay (D), because Garay (D) was financially better off, owned his own home, and had remarried.

CONCISE RULE OF LAW: Comparative income or economic advantage is not a permissible basis for a custody award.

FACTS: Burchard (P) and Garay (D) had a brief relationship during which Burchard (P) became pregnant. Garay (D) refused to believe that he was the father of the child. Burchard (P) cared for the child and worked in order to support them while training to become a registered nurse. During this time, Garay (D) denied paternity and failed to either visit the child or to provide support. Burchard (P) commenced an action to establish paternity and seeking support. Blood tests confirmed that Garay (D) was the father. He stipulated to paternity and commenced support payments. Garay (D) subsequently sought visitation rights and Burchard (P) refused, seeking exclusive custody. Garay (D) responded and sought exclusive custody as well. The court awarded Garay (D) custody on the basis that he was better positioned financially to provide continuous care to the child. In addition, Garay (D) had remarried and could provide personal care for the child, whereas Burchard (P) was forced to rely on caretakers. Last, Garay (D) was willing to provide Burchard (P) with visitation. Burchard (P) appealed.

ISSUE: In applying the "best interests" standard, must a court award custody based on one parent's economic advantage?

HOLDING AND DECISION: (Broussard, J.) No. Comparative income or economic advantage is not a permissible basis for a custody award. Where the parent with custody of the child has an insufficient income to properly care for the child, then the court should award child support, not take away custody. The trial court erred in that, in determining custody, it failed to assess the emotional ties between child and parent. In addition, the court must consider the continuity of care. An assumption that a working mother cannot provide satisfactory care is unwarranted. Reversed.

CONCURRENCE: (Bird, C.J.) The trial court abused its discretion in failing to stress the importance of continuity and stability in determining custody and in presuming that a working woman cannot adequately care for her child.

EDITOR'S ANALYSIS: The "best interests of the child" test is the test invoked in most jurisdictions. In making a determination regarding child custody, the best interests test requires the court to consider a variety of factors. These include the emotional attachment of the child to the parent, the guidance the parent provided to the child during his or her formative years, and the maintenance of continuity in custody arrangements.

NOTES:

PATRICIA ANN S. v. JAMES DANIEL S.
Mother (P) v. Father (D)
W. Va. Sup. Ct. of App., 435 S.E.2d 6 (1993).

NATURE OF CASE: Appeal from circuit court grant of custody.

FACT SUMMARY: Patricia Ann S. (P) appealed from the circuit court's granting of custody to her husband, James S. (D), on the basis that the court erred in failing to find that she was the primary caretaker of the children.

CONCISE RULE OF LAW: The primary caretaker is the natural or adoptive parent who, until the commencement of divorce proceedings, has been primarily responsible for the care and nurturing of the child.

FACTS: Patricia (P) and James (D) were married in 1967 and had three children. Patricia (P) was employed as a kindergarten teacher, but terminated her employment on the birth of their first child. James (D) was an architect. Upon the dissolution of their marriage, the circuit court granted custody of the children to James (D). Patricia (P) appealed on the basis that the circuit court erred in failing to find that she was the primary caretaker of the children; in its utilization of psychological expert testimony; and in granting custody of the children to James (D).

ISSUE: Is the primary caretaker the natural or adoptive parent who, until the commencement of divorce proceedings, has been primarily responsible for the care and nurturing of the child?

HOLDING AND DECISION: (Per curiam) Yes. The primary caretaker is the natural or adoptive parent who, until the commencement of divorce proceedings, has been primarily responsible for the care and nurturing of the child. It is presumed that it is in the child's best interest to be placed in the primary caretaker's custody. If the trial court cannot determine whether one parent has assumed such responsibility in respect to the child, then neither parent has the benefit of the presumption. In the present case, the record demonstrated that both Patricia (P) and James (D) shared the primary caretaker duties. While Patricia (P) was the homemaker and spent the majority of the time with the children during the day, the length of time spent with the children is not determinative of whether a parent should be granted the primary caretaker presumption. Moreover, the evidence showed that James (D) substantially shared the caretaker duties when he returned from work each evening. Both parties helped the children get ready for bed at night and for school in the morning, and prepared the family's meals. Both parents were involved in school organizations, helped the children with their homework, and planned the family's social activities. Last, both parents participated in the discipline of the children. Since both parties equally participated in the child care duties of the children, neither party was entitled to the primary

caretaker presumption. Thus, the determination of custody depends upon a determination of the best interests of the children. Patricia (P) challenged the circuit court's admission of the testimony of psychological experts prior to the court's determination of primary caretaker status. The circuit court determined, based on a substantial evidentiary record, that the best interests of the children required that custody be granted to James (D). The circuit court did not err in holding that the awarding of custody to James (D) would be in the best interest of the two boys. The case is remanded to determine what is in the best interests of their daughter.

DISSENT: (Workman, C.J.) The circuit court abused its discretion in allowing testimony on the question of the fitness of the parties and in denying primary caretaker status to Patricia (P). It erroneously elevated James' (D) limited hours with his children to accord him the same caretaker status as Patricia (P), a full-time stay-at-home mother.

EDITOR'S ANALYSIS: The majority of jurisdictions apply the "best interests test" in determining the custody of the child. Note that while many jurisdictions consider primary caretaking as one factor to be applied in determining the best interests of the child, West Virginia is the only jurisdiction that invokes a formal presumption in favor of a primary caretaker. The primary caretaker presumption requires that the parent who is demonstrated to be the primary caretaker of the children be awarded custody, unless it is demonstrated that he or she is unfit.

QUICKNOTES
PRIMARY CARETAKER RULE - in a custody dispute involving children of tender years, it is incumbant on the court to determine as a threshold question which parent was the primary caretaker before the domestic strife giving rise to the proceeding began.

NOTES:

IN RE MARRIAGE OF ELSER
Wife (P) v. Husband (D)
895 P.2d 619 (Mont. 1995).

NATURE OF CASE: Appeal of denial of motion.

FACT SUMMARY: In their separation agreement, Cindy Ansell (P) and Dan Elser (D) agreed that neither party would move the children to a permanent residence outside the state of Montana without the other party's written consent or the court's approval. Cindy (P) moved the court to allow her to remove the children outside of Montana and the court denied her motion. She filed this appeal.

CONCISE RULE OF LAW: Decisions regarding child custody are governed by the "best interests of the child" standard.

FACTS: Cindy (P) and Dan (D) incorporated a clause into their separation agreement that provided that neither party could remove the children outside the state of Montana for permanent residence without the written consent of the other party or the approval of the court with jurisdiction over the matter. For purposes of pursuing her career as a radiology assistant, Cindy (P) wanted to move the children to Kansas. Dan (D) refused to consent because it would make visitation costly and nearly impossible because of his work schedule and the children's school schedule. Cindy (P) moved the court to allow her to remove the children and that motion was denied. Cindy (P) filed this appeal.

ISSUE: Is it in the best interests of the children to allow their mother to move them outside the state of Montana for permanent residence?

HOLDING AND DECISION: (Gray, J.) No. Findings relating to custody modification are reviewed to determine if they are clearly erroneous. Cindy's (P) arguments that Dan (D) is not an active parent, that he could have seen the children much more than he did, and that parenting is not a priority for him ignore the applicable standard of review. Ample evidence supports the district court's findings that the removal of the children to Kansas would deprive Dan (D) of meaningful visitation. The high cost of travel, Dan's (D) work schedule and the children's school schedule would make visitation nearly impossible. Accordingly, the district court found that the move to Kansas was not in the children's best interest. We affirm.

EDITOR'S ANALYSIS: In resolving custody matters, courts primarily consider the best interests of the children. Courts will give some consideration to custodial rights of the parents, but the resolution of such matters will turn on whether or not the custodial change is in the best interests of the children.

NOTES:

BURGESS v. BURGESS
Wife (P) v. Husband (D)
913 P.2d 473 (Cal. 1996).

NATURE OF CASE: Appeal of decision in custody matter.

FACT SUMMARY: Wendy (P) and Paul (D) incorporated a clause into their mediation agreement concerning a visitation schedule that would apply in the event that the children were removed from the county. After Wendy (P) decided to move, the court issued a decision that the move was in the best interests of the children. Paul (D) appealed to the Appeals Court. The Appeals Court reversed and Wendy (P) appeals that decision.

CONCISE RULE OF LAW: In cases where the custodial parent wants to relocate the children, that party need not show that such move is necessary. Rather, the court will consider the presumptive right of the parent to change the residence of the children so long as the move would not be prejudicial to their rights or welfare.

FACTS: Wendy (P) and Paul (D) were divorced via a mediation agreement. From the outset, Wendy (P) had expressed her desire to relocate to Lancaster because it would improve her career and give the children better access to healthcare and private schools. When Wendy (P) moved the court for leave to relocate the children, the court issued a decision that the move was in the best interests of the children. Paul (D) urged the trial court to reconsider and moved for a change of custody. The trial court denied his motion. He then appealed to the Appeals Court. The Appeals Court reversed the decision of the trial court and Wendy (P) appeals that decision.

ISSUE: In custody cases involving relocation of the children, must the parent who seeks to relocate prove that such move is necessary?

HOLDING AND DECISION: (Mosk, J.) No. In custody matters in which one parent seeks to relocate the children, the trial court must consider the presumptive right of that parent to change residence so long as the move is not prejudicial to the children's rights or welfare. The trial court did not abuse its discretion in finding that the move at issue in the present case was in the best interests of the children. First, a change in custody is only warranted when the moving party can show a material change in circumstances. Public policy favors the maintaining of continuity in a child's primary caretaker. Paul (D) has failed to show any such change in circumstances. Second, it is not necessary for a parent to show that relocation is necessary. A custodial parent need only show that a change in residence would not be detrimental to the child. In making that determination, the court will consider all factors pertaining to the child's best interest. Here, the relocation would in no way have a detrimental impact on the children. They would still be able to visit with their father weekly and they would have access to better schools and healthcare. Accordingly, we reverse the decision of the Appeals Court.

EDITOR'S ANALYSIS: Courts have noted that it is unrealistic to expect custodial parents to remain in the same location forever. As with most issues in probate court pertaining to children, the standard of review is the "best interests of the children." Thus, custodial parents have a right to change residence so long as that change is not detrimental to the rights of the children.

NOTES:

54

CABAN v. MOHAMMED
Father (D) v. Mother (P)
441 U.S. 380 (1979).

NATURE OF CASE: Review of the constitutional validity of a state statute governing adoption rights.

FACT SUMMARY: Caban (D) appealed from a family court order granting Maria Mohammed's (P) petition for adoption of their two children and terminating his parental rights and challenged the constitutional validity of the statute pursuant to which the decree was ordered.

CONCISE RULE OF LAW: A state statute distinguishing between the rights of unmarried mothers and unmarried fathers is unconstitutional in violation of the Equal Protection Clause, unless it is demonstrated that such classification is substantially related to an important state interest.

FACTS: Caban (D) and Maria Mohammed (P) lived together for five years, during which time they represented themselves as husband and wife, although they never married. During that time, Maria Mohammed (P) gave birth to two children. In 1973, Maria Mohammed (P) left Caban (D) and subsequently married Kazin Mohammed (P). Maria Mohammed (P) took the children on a weekly basis to visit her mother, Gonzales, who lived one floor above Caban (D). Caban (P) saw the children each week when they visited their grandmother. In 1974, Gonzales moved to her native Puerto Rico and took the children with her. Caban (D) went to Puerto Rico to visit the children and returned with them to New York. Maria Mohammed (P) unsuccessfully sought to retrieve the children through a police order. She then commenced custody proceedings. The family court placed the children in the Mohammeds' (P) temporary custody and granted Caban (D) visitation rights. The Mohammeds (P) filed a petition to adopt the children. The Cabans (D) cross-petitioned for adoption. The surrogate granted the Mohammeds' (P) petition and terminated Caban's (D) parental rights. The New York Court of Appeals affirmed. Caban (D) appealed, challenging the constitutional validity of New York Domestic Relations Law § 111, pursuant to which the Mohammeds (P) were granted adoption. Section III required that consent to an adoption be obtained from both parents of a child born in wedlock, but only from the mother of child born out of wedlock.

ISSUE: Is a state statute, distinguishing between the rights of unmarried mothers and unmarried fathers, unconstitutional in violation of the Equal Protection Clause, unless it is demonstrated that such classification is substantially related to an important state interest?

HOLDING AND DECISION: (Powell, J.) Yes. A state statute, distinguishing between the rights of unmarried mothers and unmarried fathers, is unconstitutional in violation of the Equal Protection Clause, unless it is demonstrated that such classification is substantially related to an important state interest. New York Domestic Relations Law § 111 authorizes an unwed mother to block the adoption of her child by not granting consent. An unwed father is not provided similar authority. Moreover, the only way he can prevent termination of his parental rights is by demonstrating that the proposed adoption is not in the best interests of the child. Since the statute provides different treatment to unmarried mothers and fathers solely on the basis of sex, the determinative issue in the present case is whether such classification bears a substantial relation to an important state interest. The Mohammeds (P) contended that the role of the mother was more important to the child's development than that of the father. The record here demonstrated that an unmarried father may have a relationship with his children that is comparable to their relationship with their mother. Thus, the classifications set forth in § 111 are not justified by a difference in the importance of the respective roles of the mother and father. The Mohammeds (P) also contended that the classification is substantially related to the state's interest in encouraging the adoption of illegitimate children. They further argued that such adoptions would be hindered by having to first obtain the consent of the unwed father, who may either withhold such consent or may be difficult to locate. While the adoption of illegitimate children is an important state interest, it does not justify a gender-based classification. Since the classification in § 111 does not bear a substantial relationship to the furtherance of an important state interest, the statute is unconstitutional. Reversed.

DISSENT: (Stevens, J.) The differences in the functions of fathers and mothers from the time of conception through infancy justify a rule affording an unwed mother the sole right to consent to the child's adoption.

EDITOR'S ANALYSIS: Prior to this decision, the Supreme Court had held that a state could not presume a married father's unfitness without first providing notice and a hearing. In that case, the father had a significant parental relationship with his children and their mother. The Court continued to emphasize the importance of a significant parental relationship in subsequent cases, upholding adoption over the objection of the natural father in cases in which there was no demonstration of such a relationship.

QUICKNOTES

N.Y. DOM. REL. LAW § III - provides that consent to adoption shall be required of the parents or surviving parents of a child born in wedlock and of the mother of a child born out of wedlock.

NGUYEN v. IMMIGRATION AND NATURALIZATION SERVICE

Petitioner for citizenship (P) v. United States Immigration Agency (D)

533 U.S. 53 (2001).

NATURE OF CASE: Appeal of denial of citizenship.

FACT SUMMARY: Nguyen (P) was denied citizenship. He appealed to the Court of Appeals, but that appeal was denied. Nguyen (P) filed this appeal to the Supreme Court of the United States.

CONCISE RULE OF LAW: A federal statute governing citizenship requirements for children born out of wedlock to a U.S. citizen abroad is constitutional, despite the fact that it treats men and women differently, because it serves an important governmental interest.

FACTS: Nguyen (P) was born in Vietnam to a Vietnamese woman and a man who was a United States citizen working for a corporation in Vietnam. When Nguyen (P) was six, he moved with his father to the United States where he resided in Texas as a permanent resident. In 1992, Nguyen (P) pleaded guilty to two counts of sexual assault of a child. While he was serving his sentence, the Immigration and Naturalization Service (hereinafter, INS) (D) initiated deportation proceedings. Nguyen (P) appealed to the Board of Immigration Appeals and the Board dismissed his appeal. He later appealed to the Court of Appeals and that appeal was denied. Nguyen (P) subsequently filed this appeal to the Supreme Court of the United States.

ISSUE: Is U.S.C. § 1409 (a), the federal statute governing citizenship of children born abroad to U.S. citizens out of wedlock, constitutional given that it treats men and women differently based on gender?

HOLDING AND DECISION: (Kennedy, J.) Yes. In order to withstand equal protection scrutiny, gender-based classifications must serve an important governmental objective and the discriminatory means employed must be substantially related to the achievement of that governmental interest. Here, the statute at issue promotes two important governmental interests. The first governmental interest is assuring that a biological relationship exists. The uncontestable biological fact is that a mother must be present at birth and a father need not be. Evidence of the mother's parentage will likely be documented in a birth certificate and witnessed by several people at a hospital. A father, however, even if present at the birth, is not necessarily the father. It is clear that mothers and fathers are not similarly situated when it comes to determining parentage. As a result, Congress provided for several affirmative steps that fathers must take to show that they are biological parents of children born abroad. We find this

unremarkable given that motherhood is inherent in the birth itself and fatherhood is in no way immediately apparent.

The second important governmental interest served by this statute is the determination to ensure that the child and the citizen parent have an opportunity to a relationship that consists of a real connection between that child and the citizen parent, and, therefore, the United States. Because mothers give birth, there is at least an opportunity for a mother to develop a meaningful relationship with the child. The same is not true in the case of fathers who may not even know that their child is born. It was reasonable for Congress to impose additional requirements for the father given the ease of travel and the current willingness of Americans to live abroad. For these reasons, a mere DNA test is not sufficient to show fatherhood. A DNA test can be performed without the father's presence. Given the profound importance of the governmental objectives at issue here, Congress was well within its authority in requiring proof of an opportunity to have a genuine parent-child relationship in order to confer citizenship on a child born abroad out of wedlock.

Having addressed the fact that there are important governmental objectives at issue, we must determine if the discriminatory means employed are substantially related to the accomplishment of those objectives. We determine that they are. The basic biological differences between men and women are genuine. The principles of equal protection do not prohibit Congress from acknowledging such differences and addressing the problem at hand in a manner that is gender-specific.

DISSENT: (O'Connor, J.) We disagree with the majority because we think that there are sex-neutral alternatives for accomplishing the important governmental objectives at issue here. The primary problem with the Court's opinion is that it fails to show that the discriminatory means provided for in the statute is necessary to the accomplishment of the government's objective. We do not see that such a link exists given that there are sex-neutral alternatives that would more efficiently serve that end. The majority acknowledges that there are gender-neutral methods that could be employed and then, in turn, dismisses them as irrelevant. However, in prior cases we have found evidence of sex-neutral alternatives as persuasive reasons to reject sex-based classifications. Accordingly, we think that the majority's analysis is a departure from settled equal protection principles.

Continued on next page.

EDITOR'S ANALYSIS: This case illustrates the legal trend of bias toward mothers as custodial parents. Despite the fact that Nguyen's father had always been his primary caretaker, his father was required by statute to take several additional steps to prove his parentage. Many state and federal statutes exhibit a bias toward granting custody to mothers due to the "biological realities" the Court discusses in Nguyen.

NOTES:

4

CHAPTER 4
NONSUBORDINATION

QUICK REFERENCE RULES OF LAW

1. **Sexual Harassment of Women in the Workplace.** In order to determine whether a working environment is hostile under Title VII, the court is not limited to a determination of whether the victim suffered economic loss as a result of the alleged misconduct. (Meritor Savings Bank v. Vinson)

2. **Sexual Harassment of Women in the Workplace.** Title VII is violated when a workplace is permeated with discrimination that is sufficiently severe or pervasive so as to alter the conditions of the victim's employment, thereby creating an abusive working environment. (Harris v. Forklift Systems, Inc.)

3. **Same-Sex Harassment and Men as Victims.** In all cases of sexual harassment brought under Title VII, including same-sex cases, the petitioner must prove that he or she was subjected to conduct that was not merely tinged with offensive sexual connotations, but that the actions constituted discrimination because of sex. (Oncale v. Sundowner Offshore Services, Inc.)

4. **Battered Women Striking Back: Self-Defense.** A defendant is entitled to jury instructions regarding perfect or imperfect self-defense only after the court first concludes that the defendant killed his or her victim as a result of reasonable fear of imminent death or great bodily harm. (State v. Norman)

5. **Legal Responses to Domestic Violence.** Courts are not required to dissolve restraining orders merely because the plaintiff has requested it. The Court should consider whether objective fear can be said to exist and whether the likelihood exists of violence recurring. (Stevenson v. Stevenson)

6. **Woman Battering and Male Dominance in the Substantive Criminal Law.** In determining whether a defendant is guilty of voluntary manslaughter, the determinative test is whether at the time of the action the defendant's reason was so altered that a reasonable man of average disposition would be liable to act as a result of emotion rather than judgment. (People v. Berry)

7. **Domestic Violence and the Patriarchal State.** Congress did not have the authority to pass a statute governing intrastate activity, specifically, gender-motivated crimes, because the activity at issue was not an economic endeavor and it did not have a substantial effect on interstate commerce. (United States v. Morrison)

8. **The Legal Response to Efforts to Define Pornography As Sex-Based Discrimination.** Pornography constitutes speech entitled to constitutional protection under the First Amendment. (American Booksellers Association, Inc. v. Hudnut)

9. **Gay Marriage Is Not Marriage.** A marriage is the legal union between a man and woman. (Jones v. Hallahan)

10. **Gay Marriage Is Not Marriage.** Same-sex couples do not have a fundamental right to marriage, but homosexuals do constitute a "suspect class" for purposes of equal protection analysis. (Baehr v. Lewin)

11. **Gay Marriage Is Not Marriage.** Under its Constitution, the State of Vermont may not exclude same-sex couples from the benefits and protections its laws provide opposite-sex married couples. (Baker v. State)

12. **Lesbian Parent Is Not a Parent.** A person who is neither the biological nor legal parent of a child does not have standing to bring an action seeking visitation with that child. (In the Matter of Alison D. v. Virginia M.)

13. **Employment Discrimination Based on Sexual Orientation.** Title VII's prohibition of discrimination applies only to discrimination on the basis of gender and not to discrimination on the basis of homosexuality. (DeSantis v. Pacific Telephone & Telegraph Co., Inc.)

14. **Employment Discrimination Based on Sexual Orientation.** Homosexuality does not constitute a suspect or quasi-suspect classification subject to either a strict or heightened scrutiny standard of review. (Padula v. Webster)

15. **Employment Discrimination Based on Sexual Orientation.** In reviewing the decision of a state agency to withdraw an offer of employment on the basis that the employee is a homosexual, the court must apply the balancing test to determine the implications of the state action on the employee's right to free speech. (Shahar v. Bowers)

MERITOR SAVINGS BANK v. VINSON
Employer (D) v. Harrassed employee (P)
477 U.S. 57 (1986).

NATURE OF CASE: Review of judgment reinstating sexual harassment claim for injunctive relief and compensatory and punitive damages.

FACT SUMMARY: Vinson (P), a former employee of Meritor Savings Bank (D), commenced suit against her branch manager, Taylor (D), and the Bank (D) alleging that she had continuously been subjected to sexual harassment by Taylor (D) in violation of Title VII.

CONCISE RULE OF LAW: In order to determine whether a working environment is hostile under Title VII, the court is not limited to a determination of whether the victim suffered economic loss as a result of the alleged misconduct.

FACTS: Vinson (P), an employee at Meritor (D), worked for four years at the same branch and was promoted from the position of teller to assistant branch manager. She notified her branch manager, Taylor (D), that she would be taking sick leave for an indefinite period. She was terminated from her employment based on excessive use of her sick leave. Vinson (P) commenced suit against Meritor (D) alleging that during the course of her employment she had been subject to sexual harassment by Taylor (D) in violation of Title VII. Vinson (P) sought injunctive relief, compensatory and punitive damages, and attorney's fees. The district court concluded that the harassment was not actionable absent an effect on Vinson's (P) employment. Accordingly, it denied Vinson (P) relief, but the court of appeals reversed and remanded. The Bank (D) petitioned for certiorari, and the Supreme Court granted review.

ISSUE: In order to determine whether a working environment is hostile under Title VII, is the court limited to a determination of whether the victim suffered economic loss as a result of the alleged misconduct?

HOLDING AND DECISION: (Rehnquist, J.) No. In order to determine whether a working environment is hostile under Title VII, the court is not limited to a determination of whether the victim suffered economic loss as a result of the alleged misconduct. Sexual harassment by a supervisor of a subordinate constitutes discrimination on the basis of sex. The Bank (D) contended that the legislative intent behind Title VII was to prohibit discrimination with respect to economic loss and not psychological injury. Meritor's (D) analysis is flawed for several reasons. First, the statutory language does not restrict discrimination to economic suffering. The statute prohibits discrimination in respect to the terms and conditions of the individual's employment and is intended to encompass any unequal treatment of men and women in the workplace. Moreover, the Equal Employment Opportunity Commission (EEOC) has promulgated guidelines specifically stating that sexual harassment constitutes discrimination on the basis of sex in violation of Title VII. The guidelines demonstrate an intent that harassment causing noneconomic injury is prohibited by Title VII. Consistent with the guidelines, courts have held that a plaintiff may demonstrate a violation of Title VII by showing that such harassment created a hostile or abusive working environment. Not all sexual harassment, however, is actionable. Rather, the harassment must be sufficiently severe or pervasive to change the conditions of employment, thereby resulting in a hostile environment. Here Vinson (P) sustained her burden in demonstrating that Taylor's (D) actions created a hostile environment in violation of Title VII. Affirmed.

EDITOR'S ANALYSIS: Title VII prohibits sexual harassment in the workplace on two bases. First, the statute prohibits "quid pro quo" harassment in which an employee is required to perform sexual favors as a term of employment or advancement. Second, Title VII prohibits conditions creating a hostile or abusive working environment. The basis of a claim of sexual harassment is that the sexual advances were not welcome. This requires the court to ascertain whether the victim demonstrated conduct whereby it may be inferred that such conduct was not welcome. Such determination must be made after review of the record in its entirety, taking into account all attendant circumstances.

QUICKNOTES
TITLE VII OF THE CIVIL RIGHTS ACT OF 1964 - states that it shall be an unlawful employment practice for an employer to fail or refuse to hire or otherwise discriminate against any individual with respect to his employment because of such individual's race, color, religion, sex, or national origin.

NOTES:

HARRIS v. FORKLIFT SYSTEMS, INC.
Female manager (P) v. Employer (D)
510 U.S. 17 (1993).

NATURE OF CASE: Review of judgment for the defense in action claiming a hostile work environment under Title VII of the Civil Rights Act of 1964.

FACT SUMMARY: Harris (P), a manager at Forklift Systems (D), that its president created an abusive working environment in violation of Title VII by continuously subjecting her and other women to derogatory comments because of their sex.

CONCISE RULE OF LAW: Title VII is violated when a workplace is permeated with discrimination that is sufficiently severe or pervasive so as to alter the conditions of the victim's employment, thereby creating an abusive working environment.

FACTS: Harris (P) worked as a manager at Forklift (D) for two years. During that time, Hardy, Forklift's (D) president, often insulted her based on her gender and made her the subject of sexual innuendoes. Harris (P) complained to Hardy about his conduct, which he promised to change. During a business negotiation with one of Forklift's (D) clients, however, Hardy asked Harris (P) whether she promised to have sex with the customer. Harris (P) terminated her employment with Forklift (D) and commenced suit against the company, claiming that Forklift (D) had fostered an abusive working environment. The district court held that Hardy's conduct did not create an abusive working environment, and the court of appeal affirmed. Harris (P) appealed.

ISSUE: Is Title VII violated when a workplace is permeated with discrimination that is sufficiently severe or pervasive so as to alter the conditions of the victim's employment, thereby creating an abusive working environment?

HOLDING AND DECISION: (O'Connor, J.) Yes. Title VII is violated when a workplace is permeated with discrimination that is sufficiently severe or pervasive so as to alter the conditions of the victim's employment, thereby creating an abusive working environment. Title VII prohibits employers from discriminating against any individual on the basis of that person's race, color, religion, sex, or national origin. Such discrimination is not limited to economic discrimination, but rather encompasses the entire scope of treatment in the course of an individual's employment. This includes whether an individual is forced to work in a hostile or abusive workplace. The district court focused on whether the conduct complained of affected the victim's psychological well-being or caused her to suffer injury. The court erred in relying on that standard. While mere comments do not rise to the level of abusiveness required by the statute, an abusive working environment that does not seriously affect the victim's psychological well-being may nevertheless violate Title VII. If the environment would be reasonably perceived as either abusive or hostile, there is no requirement that the victim sustain psychological injury. In making such a determination, the court must examine all the circumstances of the workplace. While the employee's psychological well-being is relevant to that analysis, it is not the single factor to be considered. Reversed and remanded.

CONCURRENCE: (Scalia, J.) The vagueness of the statutory language required the Court to adopt an equally vague standard for determining whether a workplace constitutes an abusive working environment.

CONCURRENCE: (Ginsburg, J.) The determinative issue should be whether the discriminatory conduct unreasonably interfered with the victim's work performance. This requires the victim to demonstrate that the working conditions made it more difficult to perform and does not require the victim to show tangible reductions in productivity.

EDITOR'S ANALYSIS: The question of whether a workplace constitutes an abusive working environment is determined in the present case according to a reasonable person standard. While the majority of jurisdictions follow the reasonable person approach, a minority of the courts have applied a "reasonable woman" standard. That inquiry requires the court to ascertain whether a reasonable woman would regard the complained-of conduct to be sufficiently severe or pervasive so as to modify the conditions of her employment.

QUICKNOTES
TITLE VII OF THE CIVIL RIGHTS ACT OF 1964 - states that it shall be an unlawful employment practice for an employer to fail or refuse to hire or otherwise discriminate against any individual with respect to his employment because of such individual's race, color, religion, sex, or national origin.

NOTES:

ONCALE v. SUNDOWNER OFFSHORE SERVICES, INC.

Employee (P) v. Employer (D)
523 U.S. 75 (1998).

NATURE OF CASE: Hostile environment same-sex sexual harassment claim.

FACT SUMMARY: Oncale (P) voluntarily left his job with Sundowner (D) claiming that his reasons for leaving were sexual harassment and verbal abuse by other men in the company. He brought a claim of hostile environment sexual harassment against the company and the district court held that he had no cause of action under Title VII. Oncale (P) filed this appeal.

CONCISE RULE OF LAW: In all cases of sexual harassment brought under Title VII, including same-sex cases, the petitioner must prove that he or she was subjected to conduct that was not merely tinged with offensive sexual connotations, but that the actions constituted discrimination because of sex.

FACTS: Oncale (P) worked on an oil platform in the Gulf of Mexico for respondent, Sundowner (D). Other members of his crew physically assaulted Oncale (P) in a sexual manner. On one occasion, the crew restrained Oncale (P) and pushed a bar of soap in his anus. The crew also threatened to rape Oncale (P). Though he complained to supervisory personnel, no one responded to Oncale's (P) pleas for help with the situation. Finally, Oncale (P) left his job voluntarily because he felt he was in danger of being raped. The district court held that Oncale (P) did not have a claim under Title VII because he was of the same sex as his harassers. Oncale (P) filed this appeal to the Supreme Court of the United States.

ISSUE: Can a person who is of the same sex as his or her alleged harassers have a claim of sexual harassment under Title VII?

HOLDING AND DECISION: (Scalia, J.) Yes. Courts have taken a wide variety of stances in "hostile environment" sexual harassment cases when the victim and the alleged harasser are of the same sex. We do not think that there should be a categorical rule excluding same-sex harassment claims under Title VII. Sexual harassment need not be motivated by sexual desire to show discrimination based on sex. The petitioner need only prove that he or she was subjected to conduct that was not merely tinged with offensive sexual connotations, but that actually constituted discrimination because of sex.

EDITOR'S ANALYSIS: In its decision, the Court fails to identify exactly how Oncale could prove that he was discriminated against because of sex. Given that he and his harassers were purportedly heterosexual men working in a primarily male environment, it is not clear how such a case could be proven. Oncale must somehow show that his co-workers discriminated against him because he was a man—a seemingly impossible burden.

NOTES:

63

STATE v. NORMAN
State of N. Carolina (P) v. Battered wife (D)
N.C. Sup. Ct., 378 S.E.2d 8 (1989).

NATURE OF CASE: Appeal from judgment granting a new trial following conviction for voluntary manslaughter.

FACT SUMMARY: Mrs. Norman (D) contended that the trial court erred in not issuing a jury instruction regarding perfect or imperfect self-defense.

CONCISE RULE OF LAW: A defendant is entitled to jury instructions regarding perfect or imperfect self-defense only after the court first concludes that the defendant killed his or her victim as a result of reasonable fear of imminent death or great bodily harm.

FACTS: Mrs. Norman (D) endured a twenty-year history of beatings and other dehumanizing and degrading treatment by her husband, J.T. On June 10, 1985 he was arrested for driving under the influence. When he was released the next morning, he became extremely angry and abusive. After being beaten all day, Mrs. Norman (D) called the police, but refused to press charges because she was afraid her husband would kill her. After the police left, she tried to commit suicide by swallowing a bottle of pills. J.T. cursed her while the paramedics were attending her, and told them to let her die. After being treated at the hospital, Mrs Norman (D) went to a mental health center and social services office, where J.T. found her and made her go home with him. That night, after beating her throughout the day, J.T. made her lie on the floor while he slept on the bed. After he fell asleep, she took her child to her mother's house and took a pistol out of her purse. She shot him three times in the back of the head while he was sleeping. Mrs. Norman (D) was charged with first-degree murder. Mrs. Norman (D) presented evidence at trial that she had suffered a long history of physical and mental abuse as a result of J.T.'s alcoholism. Expert witnesses testified at trial that Mrs. Norman (D) displayed the characteristics of the battered wife syndrome, which was typified by the feeling that she could not escape the control of her husband and that law enforcement was powerless to stop him. Mrs. Norman (D) appealed and the court of appeals granted a new trial, stating that the trial court erred in refusing to consider an acquittal by reason of perfect self-defense based on evidence that Mrs. Norman (D) suffered from "battered women's syndrome." The State (P) appealed.

ISSUE: Is a defendant entitled to jury instructions regarding perfect or imperfect self-defense only after the court first concludes that the defendant killed his or her victim as a result of reasonable fear of imminent death or great bodily harm?

HOLDING AND DECISION: (Mitchell, J.) Yes. A defendant is entitled to jury instructions regarding perfect or imperfect self-defense only after the court first concludes that the defendant killed his or her victim as a result of reasonable fear of imminent death or great bodily harm. Whether the belief is reasonable is based on a determination of whether such a belief would be created in the mind of a person of ordinary sensibilities under the circumstances as they appeared to the defendant. The defendant must not have been the initial aggressor in the altercation. The right of perfect self-defense is justified under the law and is not illegal. In contrast, the right of imperfect self-defense reduces the culpability of the defendant; however, the defendant is not perceived as justified in committing the killing, so that his or her crime is reduced to voluntary manslaughter. Here Mrs. Norman (D) was not entitled to a jury instruction regarding either perfect or imperfect self-defense because she failed to introduce evidence tending to show that she reasonably perceived the killing of her husband to be necessary to prevent her imminent death or suffering of great bodily harm. Mrs. Norman (D) was not confronted with an instantaneous decision between killing J.T. or being killed herself or suffering great bodily harm. Rather, the record demonstrated that Mrs. Norman (D) had sufficient time and opportunity to employ other means of avoiding future abuse by J.T. Here the court of appeals proposed justifying the killing of another human being on the speculation that death or great bodily harm may occur at sometime in the future. This court declines to expand the scope of the immanency requirement to include such speculation. Reversed.

DISSENT: (Martin, J.) The requirement of imminence must be measured by the defendant's perception. The record in the present case demonstrated that Mrs. Norman (D) suffered continuous abuse by her husband, subjecting her to constant imminent fear of death and great bodily harm.

EDITOR'S ANALYSIS: The imminence requirement for self defense ensures that the killing is only committed when necessary and in the absence of other alternatives in order for the individual to exercise his right of self-preservation under natural law. It also ensures that the killing is justified and hence does not constitute a legal wrong. "Imminent" is defined as an immediate danger that must be confronted instantaneously and does not allow for the intervention of a third party or the law.

QUICKNOTES

IMPERFECT SELF DEFENSE - permits reduction of sentence to manslaughter when it reasonably appears to the defendant it is necessary to kill the decedent-the initial aggressor-and to save herself.

PERFECT SELF DEFENSE - permits acquittal if at the time of the killing the defendant believed it to be necessary to kill the decedent to save herself from imminent death or great bodily harm.

STEVENSON v. STEVENSON
Wife (P) v. Husband (D)
714 A.2d 986 (N. J. Super. Ct. 1998).

NATURE OF CASE: Petition to resolve final restraining order.

FACT SUMMARY: Husband (D) beat Wife (P) to the verge of death. As a result, Wife (P) obtained a restraining order. Eventually, Wife (P) sought to dissolve the restraining order and the Court refused to do so. Wife (P) appealed.

CONCISE RULE OF LAW: Courts are not required to dissolve restraining orders merely because the plaintiff has requested it. The Court should consider whether objective fear can be said to exist and whether the likelihood exists of violence recurring.

FACTS: Husband (D) beat Wife (P) so that she was bleeding from her mouth, nose and ears. She suffered a concussion and fractured ribs. Wife (P) was so severely injured that she had to be medvac'd by helicopter to a hospital. Wife (P) sought a restraining order against Husband (D) after this incident. Eventually, Wife (P) sought to dissolve the restraining order after reconsidering her relationship with Husband (D). The court refused to dissolve the order and Wife (P) filed this appeal.

ISSUE: Must a court dissolve a restraining order because a plaintiff requests it?

HOLDING AND DECISION: (Cook, J.) No. A plaintiff seeking to dissolve a permanent restraining order must show good cause to do so. In considering such a petition, the Court must consider whether objective fear can be said to continue to exist, and also whether there is a likelihood that the violence will recur. In this extreme situation, where the victim has been subjected to many beatings in the past and one severely brutal beating, the Court finds that objective fear clearly exists. Additionally, the Court notes that the facts compel the inescapable conclusion that Husband (D) will visit future beatings upon his wife should this Restraining Order be dissolved. Accordingly, we find that the Restraining Order will remain in effect.

EDITOR'S ANALYSIS: This case illustrates a legal trend in dealing with victims of domestic violence. For example, it has become common for prosecutors to proceed in cases of domestic violence without the support of the victim. The unique impact of domestic violence on the mindset of the victim has forced courts to become more proactive in dealing with such cases. The question remains whether such policies are realistic and whether they actually serve the safety of victims.

NOTES:

PEOPLE v. BERRY
State (P) v. Wife killer (D)
Cal. Sup. Ct., 556 P.2d 777 (1976).

NATURE OF CASE: Appeal from conviction of first-degree murder.

FACT SUMMARY: Berry (D) appealed from his conviction of first-degree murder for the killing of his wife, Rachel, claiming that he committed the crime while in a state of uncontrollable rage and therefore the trial court erroneously failed to give the jury an instruction as to voluntary manslaughter.

CONCISE RULE OF LAW: In determining whether a defendant is guilty of voluntary manslaughter, the determinative test is whether at the time of the action the defendant's reason was so altered that a reasonable man of average disposition would be liable to act as a result of emotion rather than judgment.

FACTS: Berry (D) and Rachel were married in 1974. Three days after their wedding, Rachel went to her native Israel, returning two months later. Berry (D) shortly thereafter choked her into unconsciousness. She reported the incident to the police department. She was interviewed by an investigator, and following the interview, a warrant was issued for Berry's (D) arrest. The following day, Berry (D) strangled Rachel to death. At trial Berry (D) did not deny murdering his wife; however, he argued that he was provoked into doing so due to a state of uncontrollable rage that was caused by provocation. Therefore, he argued, the sentence should be reduced from murder to voluntary manslaughter. The rage, he explained, was caused by Rachel's informing him upon her return from Israel that she was in love with another man and wanted a divorce. The jury found Berry (D) guilty of first-degree murder and assault likely to cause great bodily injury. Berry (D) appealed.

ISSUE: In determining whether a defendant is guilty of voluntary manslaughter, is the determinative test whether at the time of the action the defendant's reason was so altered that a reasonable man of average disposition would be liable to act as a result of emotion rather than judgment?

HOLDING AND DECISION: (Sullivan, J.) Yes. In determining whether a defendant is guilty of voluntary manslaughter, the determinative test is whether at the time of the action the defendant's reason was so altered that a reasonable man of average disposition would be liable to act as a result of emotion rather than judgment. Voluntary manslaughter is defined as the unlawful killing of another person without malice and "in the heat of passion." A finding of voluntary manslaughter does not require a specific type of provocation; mere words may suffice. The phrase "heat of passion" has been interpreted to mean not only anger or rage, but any intense emotion. Moreover, such a state may have been created by actions that took place over a period of time. In the present case, Rachel's conduct over the two-week period leading up to her death was such that would cause an ordinary man of average disposition to act without judgment. Psychiatric testimony offered at trial confirmed the statements by Berry (D) that he was in an uncontrollable rage at the time of the killing. The State (P) contended that Berry (D) could not have killed Rachel in the heat of passion since there was an adequate cooling-off period. The provocation, however, took place over a period of time during which there were periods of rage in response to specific acts of provocation. Such was the case when Berry (D) committed the killing. The trial court failed to instruct the jury as to the factual question of whether Berry (D) committed the murder while in a heat of passion resulting from adequate provocation. That failure constituted prejudicial error. Reversed.

EDITOR'S ANALYSIS: The "heat of passion" defense is based on the early common law notion that a killing committed in "the heat of passion" and with "adequate provocation" did not constitute murder with malice aforethought, but rather the lesser offense of voluntary manslaughter. In determining whether a defendant acted in the heat of passion, the court must ascertain whether the actor's reason was altered as a result of some intense emotion. There is no requirement that the emotion be the result of fear. Moreover, the desire for revenge is never adequate provocation.

QUICKNOTES

FIRST DEGREE MURDER - The willful killing of another person with deliberation and premeditation; first-degree murder also encompasses those situations in which a person is killed within the perpetration of, or attempt to perpetrate, specified felonies.

VOLUNTARY MANSLAUGHTER - The killing of another person without premeditation, deliberation or malice aforethought, but committed while in the "heat of passion" or upon some adequate provocation, thereby reducing the charge from murder to manslaughter.

NOTES:

UNITED STATES v. MORRISON

Federal Government (P) v. Alleged Rapist (D)

529 U.S. 598 (2000).

NATURE OF CASE: Certiorari review of a section of the Violence Against Women Act.

FACT SUMMARY: Morrison (D) raped Brzonkala who brought a claim against him under 42 U.S.C. Sec. 13981. The Court of Appeals determined that Congress did not have the authority to pass the statute at issue under the Commerce Clause. The Supreme Court of the United States granted certiorari review.

CONCISE RULE OF LAW: Congress did not have the authority to pass a statute governing intrastate activity, specifically, gender-motivated crimes, because the activity at issue was not an economic endeavor and it did not have a substantial effect on interstate commerce.

FACTS: Morrison (D) raped Brzonkala who petitioned for relief pursuant to 42 U.S.C. Sec. 13981, a provision of the Violence against Women Act that governed gender-motivated crimes. The District Court dismissed Brzonkala's complaint because it found that Congress did not have the authority to pass the statute at issue. A panel of the Court of Appeals reversed. However, the full Court of Appeals heard the case en banc and affirmed the District Court's ruling. The Supreme Court of the United States granted certiorari review.

ISSUE: Does Congress have the authority to pass a statute governing gender-motivated crimes given that such activity happens intrastate and is not, in and of itself, an economic endeavor?

HOLDING AND DECISION: (Rehnquist, C.J.) No. The petitioner argues that gender-motivated violence has a substantial impact on interstate commerce and, therefore, Congress had the authority to pass Sec. 13981 under the Commerce Clause. We disagree. Our decision in *Lopez* suggests that the non-economic criminal activity at issue in that case was a primary consideration in rendering our decision. In prior cases, we have found that in order for Congress to regulate an intrastate activity based on the fact of its substantial impact on interstate commerce, the activity itself must be an economic endeavor. Here, we find no basis for Congress' findings that gender-motivated violence substantially impacts interstate commerce. Accordingly, we find that Congress does not have the authority under the Commerce Clause to pass Sec. 13981.

In the alternative, petitioner argues that Congress has the power to pass the statute at issue under Sec. 5 of the Fourteenth Amendment. However, we reject this argument because we do not believe that Congress has presented evidence that bias against victims of gender-motivated crimes is present in all states or even most states. Therefore, we find that Sec. 5 of the Fourteenth Amendment does not afford Congress the authority to pass Sec. 13981.

DISSENT: (Souter, J.) We disagree with the Court's analysis because of the mountain of evidence that Congress presented proving bias against victims of gender-motivated crimes. Additionally, we disagree that Commerce Clause jurisprudence requires that the intrastate activity impacting interstate commerce be an economic endeavor.

EDITOR'S ANALYSIS: The majority is concerned that Congress will use its power to legislate under the Commerce Clause to reach almost any activity. The dissent is not worried about this, but rather, feels the Court is improperly limiting Congress' power to legislate given the "mountain" of evidence Congress presented in support of its findings for a need to exercise its power, under the Commerce Clause, to legislate gender-motivated violence.

NOTES:

AMERICAN BOOKSELLERS ASSOCIATION, INC. v. HUDNUT

Organization of 5,200 bookstores (P) v. City official (D)

771 F.2d. 323 (1985), aff'd mem., 475 U.S. 1001, reh'g denied, 475 U.S. 1132 (1986).

NATURE OF CASE: Review of constitutional validity of a city ordinance defining pornography.

FACT SUMMARY: American Booksellers Association (P) challenged the constitutional validity of a city ordinance defining pornography as a practice that is discriminatory against women.

CONCISE RULE OF LAW: Pornography constitutes speech entitled to constitutional protection under the First Amendment.

FACTS: The City of Indianapolis (D) enacted an ordinance that defined "pornography" as a practice that is discriminatory against women. The statute defined pornography as the "graphic sexually explicit subordination of women," either visually or in words that also includes women depicted as sexual objects who: 1) enjoy pain or humiliation; 2) enjoy being raped; 3) are tied up, cut up, or otherwise mutilated; 4) penetrated by either objects or animals; 5) are degraded or hurt in a sexual manner; and 6) are susceptible to domination or control. The ordinance also prohibited the depiction of men, children, or transsexuals in such manners. Supporters of the statute argued that it would reduce the view of women as sexual objects, thereby resulting in a reduction of discriminatory beliefs and practices in the workplace. Opponents (P) of the legislation argued that the statute would have the effect of suppressing much permissible speech. The district court struck down the ordinance as unconstitutional. The City (D) appealed.

ISSUE: Does pornography constitute speech entitled to constitutional protection under the First Amendment?

HOLDING AND DECISION: (Easterbrook, J.) Yes. Pornography constitutes speech entitled to constitutional protection under the First Amendment. The ordinance at issue furthers a particular view of how men and women should be depicted in sexually graphic images. So long as the speech does not portray women in positions of subordination, it is permissible. The City (D) contended that the ordinance was justified on the basis that depictions of subordination lead to the perpetuation of the subordinate positions of women, such as poorer working conditions and increased incidents of assault and rape. Such speech, however offensive, is nevertheless protected under the First Amendment. The City (D) also contended that the First Amendment does not apply to "unanswerable" speech. That argument was based on the theory that freedom of speech ensures that the truth will ultimately prevail in the marketplace of ideas; however, when the speech is unanswerable, then that guarantee is no longer viable. However, freedom of speech does not require that truth prevail. Moreover, the restriction of speech on that basis affords the government the authority to dictate what constitutes truth. That result is contrary to the principle that under the First Amendment there are no false ideas. Thus, the government may not limit speech on the basis that the truth has not yet prevailed. Furthermore, the Supreme Court has rejected the contention that speech must be "effectively answerable" in order to be afforded constitutional protection. The City (D) also contended that pornography constitutes "low value" speech and thus may be subject to regulation by the government. While courts have held that certain types of speech are not entitled to broad protection, viewpoint discrimination may not be upheld on this basis. Pornography does not constitute "low value" speech furthermore, the prohibition of certain types of pornography based on its viewpoint is not constitutionally permissible. Affirmed.

EDITOR'S ANALYSIS: Note that the court distinguished the method utilized to review "pornography" from that which utilized to review "obscenity." While pornography is subject to similar review as are other forms of discrimination, obscenity in contrast is not entitled to First Amendment protection. The standard for determining whether particular speech is obscene, is whether the publication in its entirety: 1) appeals to the prurient interest; 2) contains patently offensive demonstrations or portrayals of sexual activity as determined by community standards; and 3) the work as a whole has no "serious literary, artistic, political, or scientific value."

QUICKNOTES

IND. STAT. § 16-3 - ordinance defining pornography as discrimination redressable through administrative and judicial methods used for other forms of discrimination.

NOTES:

JONES v. HALLAHAN
Female marriage license applicant (P) v. Court clerk (D)
Ky. Sup. Ct., 501 S.W.2d 588 (1973).

NATURE OF CASE: Review of circuit court judgment denying appellants a marriage license.

FACT SUMMARY: Appellants (P) sought review of a circuit court judgment denying them the issuance of a marriage license on the basis that they were both female.

CONCISE RULE OF LAW: A marriage is the legal union between a man and woman.

FACTS: Appellants (P), two women, applied to obtain a marriage license. The circuit court held that they were not entitled to the issuance of such license, on the basis that they were both females. The appellants (P) sought review of the circuit court decision, arguing that it violated their fundamental right to marry, right of association, and the right to free exercise of religion. Appellants (P) also argued that the holding subjected them to cruel and unusual punishment.

ISSUE: Is a marriage the legal union between a man and woman?

HOLDING AND DECISION: (Vance, J.) Yes. A marriage is the legal union between a man and woman. Since the state statutes relating to the institution of marriage do not define that term, the term must be defined in accordance with its common usage. Dictionaries all define marriage as a form of legal union between a man and a woman. While the state statutes at issue do not specifically exclude same-sex marriages, they do not expressly authorize them. Traditionally, marriage has constituted a union between a man and woman, and there exists no legal authority holding otherwise. Moreover, the two other states confronted with the issue have reached the same conclusion. In the present case, the appellants (P) are not prevented from marrying by the court or by statute, but as a result of their incapability of satisfying the requirements of the marital relationship. Even had the court issued a license entitling the appellants (P) to marital status, the license would have been void. Furthermore, the refusal of the court to issue appellants a marriage license did not constitute cruel and unusual punishment, nor did it violate their rights to the free exercise of religion. Affirmed.

EDITOR'S ANALYSIS: Excluding Hawaii, with respect to gay or lesbian marriages, courts generally hold that the institution of marriage constitutes the union between a man and a woman. Courts uniformly reject the argument that such a conclusion violates the parties' fundamental right to marry under the Constitution. The Supreme Court has upheld such traditional notions of marriage as well, sustaining the validity of a state criminal statute prohibiting sodomy.

NOTES:

BAEHR v. LEWIN

Same-sex marriage license applicant (P) v.
Director of Department of Health (D)
Haw. Sup. Ct., 852 P.2d 44 (1993).

NATURE OF CASE: Appeal from grant of defense motion for judgment on the pleadings in action seeking declaratory and injunctive relief from agency denial of marriage licenses.

FACT SUMMARY: The applicant couples (P) challenged the Department of Health's (DOH) (D) denial of their applications for marriage licenses on the basis that they were of the same sex, in violation of the Equal Protection and Due Process Clauses of the Hawaii Constitution.

CONCISE RULE OF LAW: Same-sex couples do not have a fundamental right to marriage, but homosexuals do constitute a "suspect class" for purposes of equal protection analysis.

FACTS: The applicant couples (P) filed for marriage licenses with the Department of Health (DOH) (D). The DOH (D) denied the couples (P) marriage licenses on the basis that they were of the same sex. The applicant couples (P) satisfied all the requirements of the state statute, except that they be members of the opposite sex. The applicant couples (P) filed a complaint for injunctive and declaratory relief, seeking a declaration that the Hawaii Revised Statutes (HRS) § 572-1 was unconstitutional, as interpreted and applied by the DOH (D) to deny the issuance of a marriage license solely for the reason that the couple was of the same sex, in violation of the Equal Protection and Due Process Clauses of the Hawaii Constitution. The couples (P) also sought preliminary and permanent injunctions against the future application of the statute to preclude same sex marriages. Lewin (D), the director of the DOH (D), filed a motion for judgment on the pleadings, contending that the couples' (P) complaint failed to state a claim for relief. The circuit court granted Lewin's (D) motion. The applicant couples (P) appealed.

ISSUE: Do same-sex couples have a fundamental right to marriage?

HOLDING AND DECISION: (Levinson, J.) No. Same-sex couples do not have a fundamental right to marriage, but homosexuals do constitute a "suspect class" for purposes of equal protection analysis. The United States Constitution affords individuals with a right to privacy. However, the common law recognizes the right to marry, encompassed in the right to privacy, as applying only to unions between a man and a woman. The right to a same-sex marriage is neither so deeply rooted in the traditions of this nation as to violate the fundamental principles of justice, nor implicit in the concept of ordered liberty. Alternatively, the applicant couples (P) contended that such a construction of the statute denied them equal protection of the law in violation of the Hawaii Constitution. The circuit court erred in holding that homosexuals do not constitute a suspect class and that HRS § 572-1 was not subject to a strict scrutiny analysis, but only a rational basis standard of review. This court has applied strict scrutiny analysis to laws that classify persons on the basis of suspect classifications or that infringe on fundamental rights under the constitution. That analysis presumes a particular statute to be unconstitutional unless the government can demonstrate a compelling state interest for the classification. Sex constitutes a suspect category, and is therefore subject to strict scrutiny review. Thus, HRS § 572-1 is presumed unconstitutional, unless it can be demonstrated that the statute is narrowly tailored and furthers a compelling state interest. Reversed.

CONCURRENCE: (Burns, J.) The definition of sex in the Hawaii Constitution includes all aspects of an individual's sex that are "biologically fated." If heterosexuality, homosexuality, bisexuality, and asexuality are determined to be biologically fated, then the constitution most likely precludes discrimination in respect to a individual's sexual orientation by distinguishing between same-sex and opposite-sex marriages.

EDITOR'S ANALYSIS: Every other jurisdiction faced with the issue of same sex marriage has held that marriage constitutes the union between a man and a woman. Courts have uniformly rejected arguments that the states' refusal to recognize same-sex marriages constitutes a violation of the fundamental right to marriage guaranteed by the constitution or discrimination on the basis of sexual orientation. In the present case, the Court analogizes its conclusion to Loving v. Virginia, 388 U.S. 1 (1967) in which the U.S. Supreme Court struck down a state miscegenation law on equal protection and due process grounds, on the basis that such a statute implicated the suspect classification of race, thereby subjecting it to a strict scrutiny review.

QUICKNOTES

HRS § 572-1 - the section of the Hawaii Marriage Law enumerating the requisites of a valid marriage contract.

BAKER v. STATE
Same-sex couples (P) v. State of Vermont (D)
744 A.2d 864 (Vt. 1999).

NATURE OF CASE: State Constitutional claim.

FACT SUMMARY: Baker (P) is one of three same-sex couples that challenge a state statute governing marriage which denies them the right to be married because they are of the same sex. The trial court found that the statute was constitutional and Baker (P) filed this appeal.

CONCISE RULE OF LAW: Under its constitution, the State of Vermont may not exclude same-sex couples from the benefits and protections its laws provide opposite-sex married couples.

FACTS: Baker (P) is one of three same-sex couples, involved in committed relationships of lasting duration. Each of the couples was denied a marriage license, upon application, because they were ineligible under the state marriage law. The couples filed suit alleging that the denial of marriage licenses constituted a violation of the Vermont Constitution. The trial court dismissed the complaint. Baker (P) filed this appeal with the Supreme Court of Vermont.

ISSUE: Is the denial to same-sex couples of the benefits and privileges afforded opposite-sex married couples, a violation of the Vermont Constitution?

HOLDING AND DECISION: (Amestoy, C.J.) Yes. Plaintiffs argue that pursuant to Chapter I, Article 7 of the Vermont Constitution, they have a right to the common benefits and protections of the law. They maintain that the denial of a civil marriage license excludes them from many legal benefits and protections including access to a spouse's medical, life and disability insurance and many other statutory protections. We acknowledge that the framers of the Vermont Constitution intended to eliminate governmental preferments and advantages in drafting the Common Benefits Clause. In analyzing the constitutionality of the denial of marriage licenses to same-sex couples, we must consider the governmental purpose served. The State (D) argues that its purpose is to advance the link between procreation and child rearing. We are not persuaded by this argument because opposite-sex couples marry for reasons other than procreation and often marry with no intention of having children or with no ability to procreate. Furthermore, there are plenty of same-sex couples that rear children through various methods of fertilization and adoption. If the State's (D) purpose for the statute is to provide for the security of children, it plainly excludes same-sex couples that are no different from opposite-sex couples with regard to the objective of raising children together. Accordingly, we hold that plaintiffs are entitled to the same benefits and protections afforded by Vermont law to married opposite-sex couples.

CONCURRENCE AND DISSENT: (Johnson, J.) I concur with the majority's opinion; however, I dissent from its proposed remedy. I would merely enjoin the defendants from denying petitioners a marriage license based only on the sex of the applicants.

EDITOR'S ANALYSIS: Following the decision in this case, the Vermont legislature created a "civil union" status for same-sex couples. Although the "civil union" confers all of the same benefits of marriage upon same-sex couples that marriage confers on opposite-sex couples, the legislature refused to call same-sex unions, marriages. This is a significant commentary on societal perceptions of marriage and society's refusal to accept a changing concept of marriage.

NOTES:

IN THE MATTER OF ALISON D. v. VIRGINIA M.
Lesbian co-parent (P) v. Birth mother (D)
569 N.Y.S.2d 586 (1991).

NATURE OF CASE: Appeal from appellate division decision denying plaintiff visitation rights.

FACT SUMMARY: Alison D. (P), a lesbian co-parent, was denied visitation by her former partner after raising a child together for several years.

CONCISE RULE OF LAW: A person who is neither the biological nor legal parent of a child does not have standing to bring an action seeking visitation with that child.

FACTS: Alison D. (P) and Virginia M. (D) lived together for two years and decided to have a child. They agreed that Virginia (D) would be artificially inseminated. They planned for the birth of the child and agreed to share all rights and responsibilities. Virginia (D) gave birth to a boy, A.D.M. For two years, Alison (P) and Virginia (D) both cared for and made all decisions regarding A.D.M. When A.D.M. was two years and four months old, Alison (P) and Virginia (D) terminated their relationship. Alison (P) moved out of the home, which they both owned. Alison (P) and Virginia (D) agreed that Alison (P) would be able to visit the child a few times a week, and that she would continue to pay one-half the mortgage and household expenses. Alison (P) continued her visitation with A.D.M. for three years, until Virginia (D) bought her interest in the house and began to restrict Alison's (P) visits with the child. Virginia (D) subsequently ended all communication between Alison (P) and A.D.M. Alison (P) commenced suit, seeking visitation rights under Domestic Relations Law § 70. The appellate division held that Alison (P) was not a parent within the definition of the statute. Alison (P) appealed.

ISSUE: Does a person who is neither the biological nor legal parent of a child have standing to bring an action seeking visitation with that child?

HOLDING AND DECISION: (Per curiam). No. A person who is neither the biological or legal parent of a child does not have standing to bring an action seeking visitation with that child. Domestic Relations Law § 70 authorizes either parent to commence a proceeding to ensure the proper exercise of their care, custody, or control over the child. Alison (P) commenced suit pursuant to § 70 on the basis that her relationship with the child and visitation agreement with Virginia (D) afforded her with standing. Furthermore, Alison (P) claimed that she was a "de facto" parent or a parent "by estoppel." Such claims do not support a finding that Alison (P) constituted a parent within the meaning of § 70. As long as Virginia (D) is a fit parent, the court may not review a decision that she determines to be in the best interests of her child. The legislature has designated specific categories of nonparents afforded standing to seek visitation when it is determined to be in the child's best interests. Such categories do not include third parties who have developed a relationship with a child, or who have had prior relationships with a parent of the child, and who wish to continue visitation. Affirmed.

DISSENT: (Kaye, J.) The majority opinion, defining "parent" to mean only a biological parent for purposes of granting visitation rights, affects a wide scope of relationships, many of which may be necessary to a child's proper development. The majority effectively precluded the consideration of the child's best interests in a visitation proceeding, unless the party seeking visitation is the child's biological parent. The case should be remanded in order to determine whether Alison (P) stands "in loco parentis" to A.D.M. and whether the granting of visitation rights to Alison (P) would be in the child's best interests.

EDITOR'S ANALYSIS: Other jurisdictions have recognized that parties other than the child's natural parents may seek visitation rights. Such jurisdictions have established a test in order to determine whether the third party stood "in loco parentis" to the child. That test requires the party seeking visitation rights to demonstrate that he or she assumed a parental role and discharged parental responsibilities with respect to the child.

QUICKNOTES

DOMESTIC RELATIONS LAW § 70 - gives parents the rights to bring proceedings to ensure the proper exercise of their care, custody, and control of their children.

IN LOCO PARENTIS - A situation in which a person has assumed the responsibilities and obligations of a lawful parent without undergoing the legal adoption process.

DE FACTO - In fact; something which is recognized by virtue of its existence in reality, but is illegal for failure to comply with statutory requirements.

ESTOPPEL - An equitable doctrine precluding a party from asserting a right to the detriment of another who justifiedly relied on the conduct

NOTES:

DESANTIS v. PACIFIC TELEPHONE & TELEGRAPH CO., INC.

Male employee (P) v. Employer (D)

608 F.2d. 327 (9th Cir. 1979).

NATURE OF CASE: Appeal from district court's dismissal of an action for violation of Title VII of the Civil Rights Act of 1964.

FACT SUMMARY: Male employees (P) brought suit against Pacific Telephone and Telegraph (D), alleging that the company discriminated against them based on their homosexuality in violation of Title VII.

CONCISE RULE OF LAW: Title VII's prohibition of discrimination applies only to discrimination on the basis of gender and not to discrimination on the basis of homosexuality.

FACTS: Male employees (P) brought suit against Pacific Telephone and Telegraph (D), charging that the company impermissibly discriminated against them in violation of Title VII based on their homosexuality. The district court dismissed. The employees (P) appealed.

ISSUE: Does Title VII's prohibition of discrimination apply only to discrimination on the basis of gender and not to discrimination on the basis of homosexuality?

HOLDING AND DECISION: (Choy, J.) Yes. Title VII's prohibition of discrimination applies only to discrimination on the basis of gender and not to discrimination on the basis of homosexuality. The employees (P) contended that since they could establish in a trial that discrimination against homosexuals has a disproportionate impact on men, discrimination in regards to sexual preference should be deemed discrimination on the basis of sex in violation of Title VII. The application of Title VII to discrimination on the basis of homosexuality is a matter for the legislature and not the judiciary. Next the employees (P) argued that by discriminating in respect to the hiring of male homosexuals, an employer invokes different employment criteria for men and women. In that situation, however, the employer is implementing the same employment criteria for males and females in refusing to hire employees who prefer sexual partners of the same gender. Last, the employees (P) sought to extend the EEOC's holding that discrimination against an employee based on the race of his or her friends may constitute discrimination on the basis of race in violation of Title VII to mean that discrimination based on the sex of the employee's sexual partner also constitutes discrimination on the basis of sex. The record, however, failed to show that Pacific Telephone and Telegraph (D) implemented policies discriminating against employees (P) based on the gender of their friends. Instead, the employees (P) demonstrated that Pacific (D) discriminated in respect to the homosexual nature of the relationships the employees (P) had with members of the same sex. Such relationships are not entitled to protection under Title VII. Affirmed.

EDITOR'S ANALYSIS: The general rule in reviewing claims of discrimination based on homosexuality under Title VII is that discrimination on the basis of homosexuality does not constitute discrimination on the basis of sex. As a result, homosexuality is not a suspect or quasi-suspect classification entitled to heightened protection and discriminatory practices are subject only to a rational basis review. As a result, courts have rejected attempts to subject homosexuality to a strict or heightened scrutiny analysis, and have upheld the state's right to prohibit homosexual practices.

QUICKNOTES

TITLE VII OF THE CIVIL RIGHTS ACT OF 1964 - states that it shall be an unlawful employment practice for an employer to fail or refuse to hire or otherwise discriminate against any individual with respect to his employment because of such individual's race, color, religion, sex, or national origin.

NOTES:

PADULA v. WEBSTER

Special agent applicant (P) v. FBI official (D)

822 F.2d 97 (D.C. Cir. 1987).

NATURE OF CASE: Review of the constitutional validity of a Federal Bureau of Investigation's (FBI) (D) practice of refusing to hire homosexuals.

FACT SUMMARY: Padula (P) challenged the constitutional validity of the FBI's (D) refusal to hire her as a special agent solely on the basis that she was a homosexual.

CONCISE RULE OF LAW: Homosexuality does not constitute a suspect or quasi-suspect classification subject to either a strict or heightened scrutiny standard of review.

FACTS: Padula (P) alleged that the FBI (D) refused to hire her for the position of special agent solely on the basis that she was a homosexual. Padula (P) further contended that such a refusal violated both FBI (D) policy and the Equal Protection Clause. The district court rejected both charges on summary judgment. The court held that the decision of whether to hire Padula (P) was within the FBI's (D) discretion and did not violate the constitution. Padula (P) appealed.

ISSUE: Does homosexuality constitute a suspect or quasi-suspect classification subject to either a strict or heightened scrutiny standard of review?

HOLDING AND DECISION: (Silberman, J.) No. Homosexuality does not constitute a suspect or quasi-suspect classification subject to either a strict or heightened scrutiny standard of review. Padula (P) argued that homosexuality should be recognized as a suspect or quasi-suspect classification. The Supreme Court has delineated several criteria in ascertaining whether a particular classification is suspect or quasi-suspect. Such factors include whether the class has a history of discriminatory treatment and whether the group as a whole displays identifiable and immutable characteristics. Padula (P) argued that based on the above criteria, homosexuality falls within these classifications. Courts have generally rejected the contention that homosexuality constitutes a suspect classification. This court has held that there is no constitutional right to engage in homosexual activity. Furthermore, the Supreme Court has upheld the constitutional validity of state statutes criminalizing homosexual conduct. The Court held that the right to privacy in respect to marriage and procreation applies only to familial relationships and not to all sexual activity between consenting persons. In that case, the Court held that consensual sodomy does not constitute a fundamental right under the Due Process Clause since it is neither "implicit in the concept of ordered liberty," nor "deeply rooted" in the country's history and traditions. Thus, the Court upheld the statute under a rational basis review, concluding that the presumption that Georgia's citizens perceive sodomy to be immoral was a sufficient justification for the statute. Based on that conclusion, a lower court may not subsequently accord suspect or quasi-suspect status to a class whose activities may be permissibly criminalized. State action that is discriminatory on the basis of homosexuality may still be subject to a rational basis review. Here the FBI (D) rationally justified its exclusion of homosexuals on the basis that the engaging of its employees in potential criminal activities, as well as the general public attitude towards homosexuality, could adversely affect the agency's execution of its law enforcement functions. Affirmed.

EDITOR'S ANALYSIS: Suspect classifications are subject to strict scrutiny analysis and must further a compelling state interest in order to be upheld. Quasi-suspect classifications are subject to heightened scrutiny analysis and must be "substantially related to a legitimate state interest." The Supreme Court has expressly recognized that only classifications based on race, alienage, and national origin constitute suspect classifications. Similarly, the Court has held that classifications based on gender and illegitimacy only constitute quasi-suspect classifications.

QUICKNOTES

SUSPECT CLASSIFICATION - A class of persons that have historically been subject to discriminatory treatment; statutes drawing a distinction between persons based on a suspect classification, i.e. race, nationality or alienage, are subject to a strict scrutiny standard of review.

QUASI-SUSPECT CLASSIFICATION - A class of persons that have historically been subject to discriminatory treatment; statutes drawing a distinction between persons based on a quasi-suspect classification, i.e. gender or legitimacy, are subject to an intermediate scrutiny standard of review.

NOTES:

SHAHAR v. BOWERS

Prospective state attorney (P) v. State attorney general (D)

114 F.3d 1097 (11th Cir. 1997) (en banc), cert. denied, 522 U.S. 1049 (1998).

NATURE OF CASE: Review of summary judgment upholding the revocation of an offer of employment by a state agency.

FACT SUMMARY: Shahar (P), a homosexual woman, challenged the constitutional permissibility of the revocation of an offer of employment made to her by the Attorney General of the State of Georgia, Bowers (D), seeking damages and injunctive relief.

CONCISE RULE OF LAW: In reviewing the decision of a state agency to withdraw an offer of employment on the basis that the employee is a homosexual, the court must apply the balancing test to determine the implications of the state action on the employee's right to free speech.

FACTS: Shahar (P), a woman, married another woman in a ceremony performed by a rabbi of the Reconstructionist movement of Judaism. Shahar (P) did not claim that her marriage had legal effect in the State of Georgia. Bowers (D), the Attorney General of the State of Georgia, withdrew an offer of employment to Shahar (P) after learning of the marriage. Shahar (P) commenced suit against Bowers (D) seeking damages and injunctive relief. Shahar (P) claimed that the revocation of the offer was in violation of her constitutional rights to the free exercise of religion, freedom of association, equal protection, and substantive due process. Bowers (D) moved for summary judgment. Summary judgment was granted for Bowers (D). Shahar (P) appealed.

ISSUE: In reviewing the decision of a state agency to withdraw an offer of employment on the basis that the employee is a homosexual, must the court apply the balancing test to determine the implications of the state action on the employee's right to free speech?

HOLDING AND DECISION: (Edmondson, J.) Yes. In reviewing the decision of a state agency to withdraw an offer of employment on the basis that the employee is a homosexual, the court must apply the balancing test to determine the implications of the state action on the employee's right to free speech. The right to association is not absolute. When a state employee acts in a confidential relationship to his or her employer or as a spokesperson of the state, First Amendment challenges to the revocation of employment are rarely upheld if the employee is in conflict with his or her employer. This action takes place amidst an ongoing controversy in the State of Georgia regarding the right to engage in homosexual sodomy. Bowers (D) revoked the offer of employment to Shahar (P) on the basis that her decision to marry another woman amidst such controversy would interfere with the department's duty to enforce the laws of the state and would injure its public perception. Bower's (D) decision to revoke Shahar's (P) offer of employment was constitutionally permissible. Affirmed.

CONCURRENCE: (Tjoflat, J.) Shahar (P) failed to sustain her burden in demonstrating that homosexual relationships have played a critical role in the nation's history and traditions, thus entitling them to constitutional protection.

DISSENT: (Godbold, J.) Bowers (D) violated Shahar's (P) rights of intimate and expressive association under the First Amendment by not acting reasonably in revoking his offer of employment.

DISSENT: (Birch, J.) Bowers' (D) inference that Shahar's (P) homosexuality would preclude her from competently enforcing the laws of the State of Georgia are not supported by the record, and do not constitute a legitimate state interest outweighing Shahar's (P) First Amendment right to freedom of association.

EDITOR'S ANALYSIS: Note that the court evaluates Shahar's (P) challenge to the revocation of Bower's (D) offer of employment under a First Amendment analysis. Courts have held that homosexual status is entitled to First Amendment protection while homosexual conduct is not. Such a distinction, however, presumes a tendency toward homosexual conduct from a homosexual's status. The dissenting opinion rejects that presumption on the basis that such inferences are merely speculative, and do not rise to the level of a legitimate state interest outweighing Shahar's rights under the First Amendment.

QUICKNOTES

SUMMARY JUDGMENT - Judgment rendered by a court in response to a motion by one of the parties, claiming that the lack of a question of material fact in respect to an issue warrants disposition of the issue without consideration by the jury.

SUBSTANTIVE DUE PROCESS - Constitutional mandate requiring that legislation affecting an individual's life, liberty or property interests must be necessary to the advancement of a compelling state interest.

CHAPTER 5
WOMEN'S DIFFERENT VOICE(S)

QUICK REFERENCE RULES OF LAW

1. **Women as Parties, Witnesses, and Litigators.** A trial court's judgment in a divorce proceeding may be reversed on appeal due to the judge's demonstration of gender bias. (In re Marriage of Iverson)

2. **Women as Parties, Witnesses, and Litigators.** The gender bias of a trial judge requires a court of appeal to set aside his or her judgment. (Catchpole v. Brannon)

3. **Gender and Juries.** The utilization of preemptory challenges to eliminate jurors solely on the basis of gender is unconstitutional in violation of the Equal Protection Clause. (J.E.B. v. Alabama ex rel. T.B.)

4. **Women and Criminal Sentencing.** A judge may appropriately authorize a downward modification of the sentencing guidelines if the circumstances are sufficiently extraordinary. (United States v. Handy)

5. **Women and Civil Remedies.** In a proceeding for disbarment, a member may present evidence of mitigating circumstances based on extreme emotional or physical difficulties only if the member first shows through clear and convincing evidence that he or she no longer suffers from such disabilities. (In re Lamb)

IN RE MARRIAGE OF IVERSON
Wife (P) v. Husband (D)
Cal. Ct. App., 15 Cal. Rptr. 2d. 70 (1992).

NATURE OF CASE: Appeal from a trial court judgment dissolving a marriage.

FACT SUMMARY: Cheryl Iverson appealed from a trial court's judgment dissolving her marriage to George Chick Iverson, challenging the court's finding that a premarital agreement signed by the parties was valid.

CONCISE RULE OF LAW: A trial court's judgment in a divorce proceeding may be reversed on appeal due to the judge's demonstration of gender bias.

FACTS: Cheryl Iverson appealed from a trial court's judgment dissolving her marriage of 15 years to George Chick Iverson. Cheryl challenged the court's ruling that a premarital agreement signed by the parties was valid. At the trial Chick testified that he did not want to get married and communicated that intent to both Cheryl and his associates. Cheryl testified, however, that it was Chick who first proposed the topic of marriage. Cheryl further testified that the premarital agreement was read to them by Chick's attorney. Afterwards, he advised her to seek the advice of an attorney. She declined and signed the document. She never discussed the contents of the agreement with an attorney before signing it, nor did she receive any advice regarding her marital rights to any property that might be acquired during the marriage. The judge ruled that the premarital agreement was valid. Cheryl appealed.

ISSUE: May a trial court's judgment in a divorce proceeding be reversed on appeal due to the judge's demonstration of gender bias?

HOLDING AND DECISION: (Sills, J.) Yes. A trial court's judgment in a divorce proceeding may be reversed on appeal due to the judge's demonstration of gender bias. Here the trial court judge's decision was so permeated by gender bias that the court of appeal may conclude that Cheryl did not receive a fair trial. The judge reasoned that while Chick was very wealthy, Cheryl had no assets besides her physical attractiveness. The judge rejected Cheryl's contention that Chick was the one who proposed marriage, on the basis that he was already living with her after only several dates. Reversed. New trial ordered.

EDITOR'S ANALYSIS: Although such obvious instances of gender bias are rare, such bias nevertheless exists in the court system. In response, a number of jurisdictions have enacted regulations prohibiting the practice of certain forms of gender bias by attorneys. Courts have rejected the notion, however, that a judge may be recused simply on the basis that she is a woman and may be prejudiced in favor of a female litigant.

QUICKNOTES

PREMARITAL AGREEMENT - An agreement entered into by two individuals, contemplation of their impending marriage, in order to determine their rights an interests in property upon dissolution or death.

NOTES:

CATCHPOLE v. BRANNON
Burger King employee (P) v. Supervisor (D)
Cal. Ct. App., 42 Cal. Rptr. 2d 440 (1995).

NATURE OF CASE: Appeal from trial court judge's judgment in favor of defendant in a sexual harassment case.

FACT SUMMARY: Catchpole (P) appealed the trial court judge's judgment in favor of her employer, Burger King (D), in a claim of sexual harassment.

CONCISE RULE OF LAW: The gender bias of a trial judge requires a court of appeal to set aside his or her judgment.

FACTS: Catchpole (P) commenced suit, charging her employer, Burger King (D), with sexual harassment, assault and battery, and intentional and negligent infliction of emotional distress. Catchpole (P) testified that she was subjected to an abusive working environment. In order to discuss her problems with her coworkers, Catchpole's (P) supervisor, Brannon (D), requested that she come to his home. There he sexually assaulted Catchpole (P). Catchpole (P) subsequently mentioned the incident to another employee, who reported it to the assistant manager on duty. Brannon (D) was terminated the following day. Catchpole (P) stated that after Brannon's (D) termination she was further subjected to harassment in retaliation for Brannon's (D) termination. Although Catchpole (P) repeatedly complained of such conduct to Burger King (D), the company took no action. The trial court judge, sitting without a jury, entered judgment in favor of Burger King (D). Catchpole (P) appealed.

ISSUE: Does the gender bias of a trial judge require a court of appeal to set aside his or her judgment?

HOLDING AND DECISION: (Kline, J.) Yes. The gender bias of a trial judge requires a court of appeal to set aside his or her judgment. The judge's conclusion in the present case seemed to be based on female stereotypes and not on the evidentiary record. The judge presumed, contrary to the evidence, that Catchpole (P) either invited or consented to Brannon's (D) sexual advances. Moreover, the judge was indifferent to Catchpole's (P) factual claims which, although contested, were supported by corroborating testimony. Such indifference, based on Catchpole's (P) failure to resist Brannon's (D) demands, was based on stereotypical notions of gender. In addition, the court ignored the fact that Catchpole (P) was dependent upon Brannon (D) in order to retain her employment and thus remain in school. Hence, the judge's handling of the evidence was unfair, requiring this court to set aside the lower court's judgment.

EDITOR'S ANALYSIS: Note that the court declined to hold that Catchpole (P) was entitled to judgment in her favor as a matter of law. The trial court's judgment was set aside on the basis that the judge's gender bias caused him to erroneously evaluate the evidence. Thus, Catchpole (P) was deprived of her right to a fair trial, requiring the lower court's judgment to be set aside.

NOTES:

J.E.B. v. ALABAMA EX REL. T.B.
Putative father (D) v. State of Alabama on behalf of mother (P)
511 U.S. 127 (1994).

NATURE OF CASE: Appeal from trial court order determining paternity and compelling defendant to pay child support.

FACT SUMMARY: J.E.B. (D) challenged a trial court order compelling him to pay child support, alleging that the State of Alabama's (P) peremptory strikes removing all male jurors were made solely on the basis of gender in violation of the Equal Protection Clause.

CONCISE RULE OF LAW: The utilization of peremptory challenges to eliminate jurors solely on the basis of gender is unconstitutional in violation of the Equal Protection Clause.

FACTS: The State (P) filed a petition in district court on behalf of a mother and minor child for paternity and support against J.E.B. (D). A panel of thirty-six potential jurors was assembled. Three jurors were excused for cause, leaving thirty-three jurors, of which ten were male. The State (P) then used nine of its ten peremptory strikes to remove the remaining male jurors. J.E.B. (D) used all except one of his peremptory strikes to remove female jurors. The jury selected was comprised of all females. J.E.B. (D) objected to the State's (P) use of its peremptory challenges, claiming that they were exercised against male jurors on the basis of gender in violation of the Equal Protection Clause. J.E.B. (D) based his contention on the prohibition on the use of peremptory strikes to eliminate potential jurors solely on the basis of race. The trial court rejected that argument and impaneled the jury. The jury concluded that J.E.B. (D) was the father of the child and ordered him to pay support. J.E.B. (D) appealed.

ISSUE: Is the utilization of peremptory challenges to eliminate jurors solely on the basis of gender unconstitutional in violation of the Equal Protection Clause?

HOLDING AND DECISION: (Blackmun, J.) Yes. The utilization of peremptory challenges to eliminate jurors solely on the basis of gender is unconstitutional in violation of the Equal Protection Clause. Intentional discrimination on the basis of gender by the state is unconstitutional in violation of the Equal Protection Clause, especially when such discrimination serves to perpetuate stereotypical notions regarding the respective roles of men and women. The nation's history of discrimination the basis of gender is sufficient to warrant a heightened scrutiny analysis. This requires the State (P) to demonstrate an "exceedingly persuasive justification" for a gender-based classification. The issue here is whether discrimination on the basis of gender in jury selection substantially furthers the legitimate government interest in obtaining a fair and impartial trial. The State (P) argued that its decision to utilize its peremptory challenges in order to remove all men from the jury was due to the fact that men may be more sympathetic to a man involved in a paternity action. However, the State (P) may not offer as a justification stereotypical assumptions regarding the attitudes of the sexes in order to justify its discriminatory actions. Gender-based discrimination in the jury selection process harms the parties, community, and jurors by inflicting prejudice into the particular proceeding and undermining society's confidence in the judicial system. This Court has held that individual jurors have a right not to be subject to discriminatory practices in the jury selection process. Reversed.

CONCURRENCE: (O'Connor, J.) The majority's holding should be limited specifically to prohibit the government's use of peremptory challenges on the basis of gender.

CONCURRENCE: (Kennedy, J.) The Constitution requires that a jury pool adequately represent the particular community and that the jury selected the reform be impartial. The Constitution does not ensure that a party be afforded a jury composed of members of a specific race or gender.

DISSENT: (Scalia, J.) One group cannot be deprived of equal protection of the laws in the jury selection process since all groups are subject to the peremptory challenge.

EDITOR'S ANALYSIS: Note that the holding in the present case did not eliminate the use of peremptory challenges; the Court merely held that gender could not be utilized as a substitute for bias. A party may nevertheless use its peremptory challenges to wholly remove a class of persons that are subject only to a rational basis review. Moreover, a party may strike individuals based on a factor that disproportionately impacts members of one sex, unless the opposing party can demonstrate that such strikes were motivated by a discriminatory intent.

QUICKNOTES
VOIR DIRE - Examination of potential jurors on a case.

PEREMPTORY STRIKE - The exclusion by a party to a lawsuit of a prospective juror without the need to specify a particular reason.

PROPTER DEFECTUM SEXUS - On account of a defect in sex.

UNITED STATES v. HANDY
Federal government (P) v. Indicted co-conspirator (D)
752 F. Supp. 561 (E.D.N.Y.1990).

NATURE OF CASE: Appeal from an indictment charging defendants with conspiring to distribute and possess with the intent to distribute cocaine.

FACT SUMMARY: Handy (D), a thirty-six year old mother of three, pled guilty to an indictment charging her with conspiring to distribute and possess with the intent to distribute cocaine.

CONCISE RULE OF LAW: A judge may appropriately authorize a downward modification of the sentencing guidelines if the circumstances are sufficiently extraordinary.

FACTS: Handy (D) was a thirty-six year old woman from Baltimore. She was one of ten children whose parents were both deceased when Handy (D) was at a young age. Handy (D) was also the single mother of three children. Handy's (D) three children reside with her and she has no prior criminal history. Moreover, she has been employed for the past thirteen years, eight of those years with Farm Fresh Food, Inc. Handy's (D) boyfriend of five years, Johnson (D), asked her to accompany him to New York City so that he may purchase drugs. Handy (D) agreed and carried the purchase money totaling $75,000 in her handbag along with a dilutent and some glassine envelopes. Handy (D) denied ever having been involved in a drug transaction with Johnson (D) before, although she was aware of his involvement in some illegal activity. Handy (D) pled guilty to a single count of conspiracy to distribute and possess with the intent to distribute cocaine.

ISSUE: May a judge appropriately authorize a downward modification of the sentencing guidelines if the circumstances are sufficiently extraordinary?

HOLDING AND DECISION: (Glasser, J.) Yes. A judge may appropriately authorize a downward modification of the sentencing guidelines if the circumstances are sufficiently extraordinary. The circumstances of the present case in respect to Handy's (D) familial relationships and employment record justify a downward departure from the sentencing guidelines for several reasons. Such factors include the fact that Handy (D) as a single mother has been continuously employed for thirteen years and that her children's future would be jeopardized due to a prolonged period of imprisonment. The issue of whether to grant a downward departure from the sentencing guidelines must be made according to the particular circumstances of the case.

EDITOR'S ANALYSIS: The court distinguishes its holding in the present case as not signifying that every case involving a single parent, or an individual with a steady employment record, warrants a downward departure from the sentencing guidelines. Furthermore, the facts that Handy (D) was from a poor socio-economic background and that she had no prior criminal history also were not relevant to the court's determination. Prior to the enactment of sentencing guidelines, judges generally considered the defendant's particular circumstances in ascertaining the appropriate term of punishment. The sentencing guidelines prohibit the court from considering such personal factors except in extraordinary cases, and expressly exclude the consideration of familial responsibilities from that determination.

NOTES:

IN RE LAMB

Impersonator (D)

Cal. Sup. Ct., 776 P.2d 765 (1989).

NATURE OF CASE: Review of state bar decision recommending disbarment.

FACT SUMMARY: Laura Beth Lamb (D) sought review of a decision of the State Bar of California recommending her disbarment based on her conviction of two felony counts of false impersonation to obtain a benefit, for taking the July 1985 bar examination in her husband's place.

CONCISE RULE OF LAW: In a proceeding for disbarment, a member may present evidence of mitigating circumstances based on extreme emotional or physical difficulties only if the member first shows through clear and convincing evidence that he or she no longer suffers from such disabilities.

FACTS: Lamb (D) was admitted to practice before the State Bar of California in 1983. In 1985, she posed as her husband, Morgan Lamb, in a photograph which she submitted to the State Bar as identification in order to take the July 1985 bar examination. She then took the examination in her husband's place. In 1986, she pled nolo contendere to two felony counts of false impersonation. Lamb (D) was convicted and the matter referred to the State Bar for a determination of the appropriate discipline. The hearing officer recommended that Lamb (D) be disbarred and the review department affirmed. Lamb (D) sought review, arguing that the emotional problems that had caused her misconduct had been alleviated.

ISSUE: In a proceeding for disbarment, may a member present evidence of mitigating circumstances based on extreme emotional or physical difficulties only if the member first shows through clear and convincing evidence that he or she no longer suffers from such disabilities?

HOLDING AND DECISION: [Per curiam.] Yes. In a proceeding for disbarment, a member may present evidence of mitigating circumstances based on extreme emotional or physical difficulties only if the member first shows through clear and convincing evidence that he or she no longer suffers from such disabilities. In this case, Lamb (D) contended that her misconduct was the result of extreme physical and psychological pressures. While the Standards for Attorney Sanctons for Professional Misconduct provide that such disabilities may sometimes serve as mitigating circumstances, due to the public's interest in protecting against unfit members, Lamb (D) was required to present clear and convincing evidence of her complete recovery and rehabilitation. Lamb (D) failed to sustain her burden. Thus, it cannot be determined that Lamb (D) would not act similarly in the future. Lamb (D) may demonstrate evidence of such

rehabilitation in a petition for reinstatement. The State Bar Court's recommendation for disbarment is adopted.

DISSENT: (Kaufman, J.) The circumstances giving rise to Lamb's (D) misconduct were the result of conditions that no longer exist. The primary purpose of disciplinary measures by the State Bar is in order to protect the public and not the punishment of the individual attorney. In the present case, since Lamb (D) no longer poses a danger to the public, her disbarment is only punitive. A better alternative would be to impose conditions of probation upon Lamb (D) that would be tailored to ensure that she be rehabilitated and the public protected.

EDITOR'S ANALYSIS: A recommendation of disbarment for conduct involving acts of moral turpitude may only be overturned by a court if the member shows evidence of his or her complete and sustained rehabilitation. In the present case, the hearing officer proposing Lamb's (D) disbarment stated that because her crimes involved moral turpitude, disbarment was required, unless Lamb (D) could show the most compelling mitigating circumstances. Based on the severity of Lamb's (D) conduct, the recommendation for disbarment may not be overturned without a demonstration of complete and sustained rehabilitation.

QUICKNOTES

DISBARMENT - The suspension of an attorney's license to practice law by a court for unlawful or unethical behavior.

MORAL TURPITUDE - Intentional conduct demonstrating depravity or vileness and which is contrary to acceptable and traditional societal behavior.

NOTES:

CHAPTER 6
AUTONOMY

QUICK REFERENCE RULES OF LAW

1. **"Statutory" Rape: The (Ir)Relevance of Consent.** A state statute making only males criminally liable for having sexual relations with a minor female does not violate equal protection. (Michael M. v. Superior Court of Sonoma County)

2. **Rape: Distinguishing Consent and Nonconsent.** In a rape proceeding, a defendant must be granted an opportunity to show that, in the context of his particular case, the probative value of otherwise inadmissible evidence outweighs its prejudicial effect on the victim. (State v. Colbath)

3. **Marital Rape.** In order to sustain a conviction of marital rape, the prosecution must establish beyond a reasonable doubt both the violation of the general rape statute and that the wife unilaterally had revoked her implied consent to marital intercourse. (Kizer v. Commonwealth of Virginia)

4. **Control of Conception and Other Aspects of Women's Health.** Marriage constitutes a privacy right guaranteed by the Fourth Amendment. (Griswold v. Connecticut)

5. **Control of Conception and Other Aspects of Women's Health.** A state statute according different treatment to married and unmarried persons is unconstitutional, unless the state can demonstrate a rational basis for the distinction. (Eisenstadt v. Baird)

6. **Control of Conception and Other Aspects of Women's Health.** A company's choice to exclude a prescription drug used only by women from its generally applicable benefit plan constitutes sex discrimination and is actionable under Title VII. (Erickson v. Bartell Drug Co.)

7. **Abortion: The Legal Framework.** Women have the right to terminate pregnancy up until the point in time at which the fetus is capable of meaningful life outside the mother's womb. (Roe v. Wade)

8. **Abortion: The Legal Framework.** Only where state regulation imposes an undue burden on a woman's ability to procure an abortion does the power of the state violate the liberty interest protected by the Due Process Clause. (Planned Parenthood of Southeastern Pennsylvania v. Casey)

9. **Pregnancy and Contractual Autonomy.** Under a surrogate-parenting contract, once conception occurs, the parties' rights in respect to the child are fixed, and may only be altered upon a demonstration that such modification is in the best interests of the child. (In re Baby M)

10. **The Pregnant Woman and Fetus as Adversaries.** Screening the urine of pregnant women for drugs in order to provide for the safety of the fetus does not constitute a "special need" divorced from the purpose of law enforcement where the primary goal of the search is to use its fruits to coerce the subjects of the search into treatment through the threat of law enforcement. (Ferguson v. City of Charleston)

MICHAEL M. v.SUPERIOR COURT OF SONOMA COUNTY
Convicted rapist (D) v. Court (P)
450 U.S. 464 (1981).

NATURE OF CASE: Appeal from conviction for statutory rape.

FACT SUMMARY: Michael M. (D) contended a state statutory rape law violated equal protection because it discriminated on the basis of gender in making males only criminally liable.

CONCISE RULE OF LAW: A state statute making only males criminally liable for having sexual relations with a minor female does not violate equal protection.

FACTS: Michael M. (D) was convicted of statutory rape for having sexual relations with a 15-year-old girl. He was 17½ at the time of the act, and the statute made men alone criminally liable. A female having sexual relations with a male under the age of 18 could not be guilty of statutory rape. Michael (D) appealed, contending the statute violated equal protection. The California Court of Appeal and Supreme Court affirmed the conviction, and the U.S. Supreme Court granted certiorari.

ISSUE: Does a state statute making only males criminally liable for having sexual relations with a minor female violate equal protection?

HOLDING AND DECISION: (Rehnquist, J.) No. A state statute making only males criminally liable for having sexual relations with a minor female does not violate equal protection. Young males are not similarly situated with young females in questions of human reproduction. The young female bears the greatest physical, emotional, and oftentimes financial burden of pregnancy. Thus, the need to protect them is greater. Therefore, because the prevention of teenage pregnancy is a legitimate state interest and this statute bears a fair relationship to that end, the statute is constitutional. Affirmed.

CONCURRENCE: (Blackmun, J.) The California statutory rape law is a sufficiently reasoned and constitutional effort to control the problem of teenage pregnancy at its inception. Further, California's efforts to prevent teenage pregnancy are to be viewed differently from Utah's efforts to inhibit a woman from dealing with pregnancy once it has become an inevitability.

DISSENT: (Brennan, J.) This statute is clearly gender based and as such must bear a substantial relationship to the state goal sought to be achieved. It does not and is invalid.

DISSENT: (Stevens, J.) This statute will not curtail teenage pregnancy. However, a nondiscriminatory prohibition against teenage sexual relations would be constitutional.

EDITOR'S ANALYSIS: This statute, while clearly rooted in the tradition of the common law, clearly has a modern approach to the burgeoning problem of teenage pregnancies. It also seeks to curtail venereal disease and as such is directly related to an important state interest. Gender-based classifications have not as yet been held to be suspect classifications warranting the application of a strict scrutiny standard of review for such legislation.

QUICKNOTES
CAL. PENAL CODE ANN. § 261.5 - defines unlawful sexual intercourse as an act of sexual intercourse accomplished with a female not the wife of the perpetrator, where the female is under the age of eighteen years.

NOTES:

STATE v. COLBATH

State of New Hampshire (P) v. Convicted rapist (D)

N.H. Sup. Ct., 540 A.2d 1212 (1988).

NATURE OF CASE: Appeal from trial court judgment convicting defendant of rape.

FACT SUMMARY: Colbath (D) appealed from a jury finding that he was guilty of rape on the basis that the trial court judge improperly instructed the jury that evidence of the complainant's behavior with other men was irrelevant to the determination of Colbath's (D) innocence.

CONCISE RULE OF LAW: In a rape proceeding, a defendant must be granted an opportunity to show that, in the context of his particular case, the probative value of otherwise inadmissible evidence outweighs its prejudicial effect on the victim.

FACTS: Colbath (D) went to the Smokey Lantern with some friends, where he met the complainant. She had directed sexually provocative attention toward several men in the bar that afternoon, including Colbath (D). The two left the bar and went to Colbath's (D) trailer, where they engaged in sexual intercourse. Colbath's (D) girlfriend came home and discovered them. She assaulted the complainant, who subsequently accused Colbath (D) of rape. Colbath (D) was arrested and charged. The trial focused on the defense of consent. The trial court judge instructed the jury that evidence of complainant's behavior with other men was irrelevant to the issue of whether she consented to sexual intercourse in the present case. The jury returned a verdict of guilty. Colbath (D) appealed, arguing that the New Hampshire rape shield law should not apply to evidence of consensual sexual activity with others that occurs in a public place.

ISSUE: In a rape proceeding, must a defendant be granted an opportunity to show that, in the context of his particular case, the probative value of otherwise inadmissible evidence outweighs its prejudicial effect on the victim?

HOLDING AND DECISION: (Souter, J.) Yes. In a rape proceeding, a defendant must be granted an opportunity to show that, in the context of his particular case, the probative value of otherwise inadmissible evidence outweighs its prejudicial effect on the victim. The New Hampshire rape shield law prohibits the admission of evidence of prior consensual sexual conduct between the victim and any other person, excluding the defendant. However, the rape shield law's terms are necessarily limited by a defendant's state and federal constitutional rights to confront witnesses against him and to present evidence that may exonerate him. In that case, the defendant must be permitted to show that the probative value of such evidence outweighs its prejudicial effect on the victim. In the present case, once such relative weight is assigned to the evidence, the public nature of the victim's conduct proves to be substantially probative. First, the prejudicial effect of describing the victim's conduct in public has less danger of being offensive than does the description of private sexual behavior behind closed doors. Second, the public display of interest in sexual activity may infer a general receptiveness to sexual advances that cannot be similarly inferred from evidence of private sexual conduct with one particular partner. Since there was little danger of violating the complainant's privacy interest, or of the evidence having a prejudicial effect, the trial court erred in preventing Colbath (D) from presenting evidence of the complainant's conduct immediately prior to the alleged rape. In this case, the Colbath's (D) constitutional right to present evidence outweighed its potential prejudicial effect. Reversed and remanded.

EDITOR'S ANALYSIS: The majority of jurisdictions have passed "rape shield laws" such as the one in the present case. Rape shield laws were enacted for the purposes of protecting the rape victim, while still convicting the alleged rapist. Federal Rule of Evidence 413 was enacted in 1994, providing an exception to the prohibition on the admissibility of evidence of prior acts to show that the defendant acted in conformity with such conduct in the present case. Rule 413 permits the admission of evidence of the defendant's prior instances of sexual violence in a federal action for sexual assault, even if it is only introduced to show the defendant's propensity to act in conformity with such conduct.

QUICKNOTES

NEW HAMPSHIRE RAPE SHIELD LAW - bars evidence of prior consensual sexual activity between the victim and anyone other than the defendant.

RULING IN LIMINE - Ruling by the court on a motion by one party brought prior to trial to exclude the potential introduction of highly prejudicial evidence.

NOTES:

KIZER v. COMMONWEALTH OF VIRGINIA
Convicted rapist (D) v. State (P)
Va. Sup. Ct., 321 S.E.2d 291 (1984).

NATURE OF CASE: Appeal from conviction of rape.

FACT SUMMARY: Edward Kizer (D) appealed from a conviction of marital rape on the basis that the prosecution failed to establish beyond a reasonable doubt the elements of the offense.

CONCISE RULE OF LAW: In order to sustain a conviction of marital rape, the prosecution must establish beyond a reasonable doubt both the violation of the general rape statute and that the wife unilaterally had revoked her implied consent to marital intercourse.

FACTS: Edward Kizer (D) and his wife, Jeri, were married in 1981. Jeri gave birth to a child. The couple began experiencing marital problems. Jeri went to Texas to visit her parents for two weeks. In February of 1983, Edward (D), who was enlisted in the Navy, moved out of the marital residence and back to his ship. Jeri testified that the couple separated at that point and that she did not wish to be married any longer. Edward (D) contended that they were not legally separated and that he only moved so that their child would not be subjected to their arguing. The record showed that the couple did not engage in sexual intercourse from the time of Jeri's visit with her parents to the date of the alleged assault. Prior to the alleged assault, Edward (D) filed a petition for custody of their son. On the day of the incident, Edward (D) was visiting friends in an apartment across the hall from Jeri. Edward (D) knocked on the door and asked to use the shower. Jeri refused, not wanting to be alone with Edward (D), and Edward (D) kicked the door down. He then picked up Jeri, carried her into the bedroom, and raped her. Following the attack, Jeri ran from the apartment and reported the incident to a police officer. Edward (D) was arrested later that day and confessed to the acts. Three weeks later, before the rape proceedings, Edward (D) was awarded custody of their son. Edward (D) was found guilty of rape and sentenced to twenty years' imprisonment. Edward (D) appealed.

ISSUE: In order to sustain a conviction of marital rape, must the prosecution establish beyond a reasonable doubt both the violation of the general rape statute and that the wife unilaterally revoked her implied consent to marital intercourse?

HOLDING AND DECISION: (Compton, J.) Yes. In order to sustain a conviction of marital rape, the prosecution must establish beyond a reasonable doubt both the violation of the general rape statute and that the wife unilaterally revoked her implied consent to marital intercourse. Such revocation of consent must be shown by a clear intent to end the marital relationship. In order to establish such an intention, the prosecution may demonstrate that the wife and husband lived separate and apart, that the wife refrained from voluntary sexual intercourse with her husband, and that the wife has acted in a manner demonstrating that the marriage has in fact ended, taking into account the surrounding circumstances. Here, the record demonstrated that Edward (D) and Jeri lived separate and apart, and that Jeri refrained from engaging in voluntary sexual intercourse with Edward (D) for six months. However, the prosecution failed to prove that Jeri acted in a manner evidencing an end to the marriage in fact. While Jeri subjectively considered the marriage to be over, she did not manifest that intent to Edward (D). Moreover, Jeri acted in such an ambiguous manner that Edward (D) could not have reasonably perceived that the marriage was terminated. Reversed.

DISSENT: (Thomas, J.) The majority inserted a new element to the offense of marital rape by requiring that the wife demonstrate a manifest intent to terminate the marital relationship as determined from the husband's perspective. Prior case law only required that an objective party be able to determine that the wife acted in such a manner as to indicate the termination of the marriage. Moreover, the fact that Edward (D) filed for custody of their child further demonstrates the fact that he considered their marriage to have ended. Thus, the pendency of the custody suit added to the six-month absence of sexual relations and the one-month separation would lead any objective observer to conclude that the marriage was at an end.

EDITOR'S ANALYSIS: Note that the termination of the marital relationship must be manifested in accordance with an objective, and not a subjective, viewpoint. The court distinguished the present case from Weishaupt v. Commonwealth, 315 S.E.2d 847 (Va. 1984), the case relied on by the prosecution. In that case, the wife moved out of the marital residence and the parties lived separate and apart for eleven continuous months, during which time there was no contact between the husband and wife and the wife consulted a divorce attorney. There the court determined that the wife's intent was unequivocal as judged from an objective viewpoint, and the prosecution had thus sustained its burden in showing beyond a reasonable doubt that the husband knew, or reasonably should have known, that the marriage had ended in fact.

GRISWOLD v. CONNECTICUT

Planned Parenthood personnel (D) v. State (P)

381 U.S. 479 (1965).

NATURE OF CASE: Review of convictions for violation of a state law banning the use of contraceptives.

FACT SUMMARY: Employees (D) of Planned Parenthood who had prescribed contraceptives to married couples were charged as accessories to the violation of a Connecticut statute that prohibited the use of contraceptives.

CONCISE RULE OF LAW: Marriage constitutes a privacy right guaranteed by the Fourth Amendment.

FACTS: Employees (D) of Planned Parenthood prescribed contraceptives to married couples as part of their employment duties. The employees (D) were charged as accessories to the violation of a Connecticut state statute that prohibited the use of contraceptives. Their subsequent convictions were upheld by the lower courts. The Supreme Court granted review.

ISSUE: Does marriage constitute a privacy right guaranteed by the Fourth Amendment?

HOLDING AND DECISION: (Douglas, J.) Yes. Marriage constitutes a privacy right guaranteed by the Fourth Amendment. The Court has consistently upheld particular rights that were not expressly granted by the Constitution. The Bill of Rights contains specific guarantees that do not have definite boundaries. Such guarantees give rise to "zones of privacy" upon which the government may not intrude. The Fourth and Fifth Amendments have been construed by this Court as protecting against invasions of the home and privacy by the government. Furthermore, this Court has held that the Fourth Amendment guarantees individuals a right to privacy. Here the prohibition on the use of contraceptives has a deleterious effect on the marital relationship, which lies within the zone of privacy guaranteed by the Fourth Amendment. Thus, the state statute is unconstitutional. Reversed.

CONCURRENCE: (Goldberg, J.) Marriage constitutes a fundamental right under the Constitution which is protected from infringement by the states. However, the majority's holding in the present case does not interfere with the states' rights to regulate sexual misconduct.

EDITOR'S ANALYSIS: Note that the Court declined to hold the state statute unconstitutional in the present case on the basis that it constituted an impermissible infringement on the economic, business, or social relationships. Rather, the Court recognized the marital relationship as falling within the fundamental right of privacy guaranteed by the Fourth Amendment and made applicable to the states through the operation of the Fourteenth Amendment. The Court describes such rights as analogous to "penumbras," thereby according them the flexibility to adapt to the changing needs of society.

NOTES:

EISENSTADT v. BAIRD
State official (D) v. Contraceptive exhibitor (P)
405 U.S. 438 (1972).

NATURE OF CASE: Review of the constitutional validity of a state statute prohibiting the dispensing of contraceptives.

FACT SUMMARY: The State (D) appealed from the decision of the Massachusetts Supreme Judicial Court, holding unconstitutional a state statutory scheme that made it unlawful for unmarried, and not married, persons to obtain contraceptives.

CONCISE RULE OF LAW: A state statute according different treatment to married and unmarried persons is unconstitutional, unless the state can demonstrate a rational basis for the distinction.

FACTS: Baird (P) was convicted of the exhibition of contraceptive devices in the course of a lecture on contraception that he gave to a group of students at Boston University. He was also convicted for giving a student a package of contraceptive foam. The Massachusetts state statute, under which Baird (P) was convicted, imposed a maximum five-year sentence for persons who distribute any form of contraceptive, except under certain circumstances. The Massachusetts Supreme Judicial Court held that the statute made it a felony for any person, other than a registered physician or pharmacist as specified, to dispense contraceptives. The court set aside Baird's (P) conviction as to the exhibition of the contraceptives, but sustained the conviction for distributing the foam to the student. Baird (P) obtained a writ of habeas corpus in federal court. The State (D) appealed

ISSUE: Is a state statute according different treatment to married and unmarried persons unconstitutional, unless the state can demonstrate a rational basis for the distinction?

HOLDING AND DECISION: (Brennan, J.) Yes. A state statute according different treatment to married and unmarried persons is unconstitutional, unless the state can demonstrate a rational basis for the distinction. The statute at issue in the present case distinguishes between the classes of persons to whom contraceptives may be distributed. Married persons may receive contraceptives by prescription from doctors or druggists in order to prevent contraception, while single persons are absolutely prohibited from obtaining contraceptives for such purposes. However, the statute permits either married or single persons to receive contraceptives from any person in order to prevent disease. The legislature's intent in enacting the statute was to deter premarital sexual activity and to regulate the distribution of contraceptives. But such interests do not provide a rational basis to uphold the statute's distinction between married and unmarried persons. The statute cannot be upheld as a deterrent to fornication or as a health measure. Nor can it be sustained as a prohibition on contraceptive because the state (D) could not, consistently with the Equal Protection Clause, outlaw distribution to unmarried but not to married persons. Affirmed.

EDITOR'S ANALYSIS: Note that the Court uses this case to expand the scope of its prior decision, Griswold v. Connecticut, 381 U.S. 479 (1965), striking down a statutory scheme which prohibited the use of contraceptives. In the prior case, the Court sustained the right of married persons to obtain contraceptives as inherent in the right of privacy accorded to the marital relationship. In the present case, the Court stated that the right of the individual to be free from government intrusions into such personal matters as the decision to have a child necessarily applied to both married and unmarried persons.

QUICKNOTES
WRIT OF HABEAS CORPUS - A proceeding in which a defendant brings a writ to compel a judicial determination of whether he is lawfully being held in custody.

NOTES:

ERICKSON v. BARTELL DRUG CO.

Employee (P) v. Employer (D)

141 F. Supp. 2d 1266 (W.D. Wash. 2001).

NATURE OF CASE: Title VII action.

FACT SUMMARY: This case is a class action on behalf of Erickson (P) and other female employees of Bartell Drug Co. (hereinafter, Bartell) (D) who were taking prescription contraceptives while on the company's Prescription Benefit Plan. The Plan denied coverage for prescription birth control.

CONCISE RULE OF LAW: A company's choice to exclude a prescription drug used only by women from its generally applicable benefit plan constitutes sex discrimination and is actionable under Title VII.

FACTS: Erickson (P) brought a Title VII claim against Bartell Drug Co. (D) alleging that the exclusion of prescription contraceptives from the company's comprehensive prescription plan constitutes sex discrimination. The suit is proceeding before the District Court as a class action on behalf of Erickson (P) and other female employees who were enrolled in Bartell's (D) Prescription Benefit Plan while taking prescription contraceptives.

ISSUE: Is a company's decision not to cover prescription drugs, used only by women, sex discrimination and actionable under Title VII?

HOLDING AND DECISION: (Lasnik, J.) Yes. Congress has adopted a broad interpretation of Title VII that requires employers to treat both sexes the same even if such treatment requires the provision of women-only benefits or the incurring of additional expenses by the company. The law now recognizes that women can bear children and men cannot and that, as a result of biology, men and women have different healthcare and disability needs. Women's healthcare needs resulting from unique sex-based characteristics must be met to the same extent as other healthcare needs. In the case at bar, Bartell (D) has chosen to provide a benefit to its employees which excludes the coverage of services that are available only to women. In doing so, Bartell (D) discriminated against female employees on the basis of their sex.

EDITOR'S ANALYSIS: This case illustrates that it is a fairly recent phenomenon for courts and lawmakers alike to acknowledge that women deserve to receive healthcare benefits that address their unique biological needs. The broader interpretation of Title VII, which Congress chose to adopt in enacting the Pregnancy Discrimination Act, has gone a long way in gaining equal treatment of women with respect to health and disability benefits in the workplace.

NOTES:

ROE v. WADE
Single pregnant woman (P) v. Agent of the State of Texas (D)
410 U.S. 113 (1973).

NATURE OF CASE: Abortion rights case.

FACT SUMMARY: Roe (P) sought an abortion in violation of a Texas criminal statute. She seeks a declaratory judgment that the statute is unconstitutional from the Supreme Court of the United States.

CONCISE RULE OF LAW: Women have the right to terminate pregnancy up until the point in time at which the fetus is capable of meaningful life outside the mother's womb.

FACTS: Roe (P) is a single pregnant woman who would like to obtain an abortion. A Texas statute criminalizes the termination of pregnancy except in cases where abortion is necessary to save the mother's life. Roe (P) seeks a declaratory judgment that the statute is unconstitutional from the Supreme Court of the United States.

ISSUE: Is a Texas statute criminalizing abortion, except in cases where it is necessary to save the mother's life, constitutional?

HOLDING AND DECISION: (Blackmun, J.) No. Although there is no explicit mention of a right to privacy in the Constitution, this Court has previously found that such a right exists. The right to privacy has been identified as originating from the First, Fourth, Fifth and Fourteenth Amendments, as well as the Bill of Rights. The right of privacy extends only to "fundamental" or "personal" rights. We think that the right to privacy is based in the Fourteenth Amendment, and that the right of privacy extends to a woman's decision whether or not to terminate her pregnancy. We do find, however, that a state has an interest in the potentiality of human life. Additionally, we find that that interest becomes a compelling interest when the fetus reaches the point of viability. That is to say, the state has a compelling interest in a fetus that is capable of meaningful life outside of its mother's womb. Accordingly, we find that a state can regulate abortion. However, we think that the Texas statute providing for abortion only when it is necessary to save a mother's life is an unconstitutional infringement upon a mother's right to privacy.

EDITOR'S ANALYSIS: *Roe v. Wade* is often held out as the case that ensures a woman's right to abortion. However, the Court's language is quite clear that a woman does not have a right to abortion. Instead, the state has no right to interfere with her decision to terminate her pregnancy up until the point that her fetus becomes capable of meaningful life outside the womb. It is important to note that the decision turns on the viability of the fetus. Thus, it is possible that it will lose its impact as medical technology advances and fetuses become "viable" at earlier stages in pregnancy.

NOTES:

PLANNED PARENTHOOD OF SOUTHEASTERN PENNSYLVANIA v. CASEY
Abortion provider (P) v. State official (D)
505 U.S. 833 (1992).

NATURE OF CASE: Appeal from a ruling reversing in part and affirming in part a finding that certain provisions of a state statute were unconstitutional.

FACT SUMMARY: Planned Parenthood (P) argued that certain provisions in Pennsylvania's (D) Abortion Control Act violated the due process and liberty spheres of the Fourteenth Amendment to the Constitution.

CONCISE RULE OF LAW: Only where state regulation imposes an undue burden on a woman's ability to procure an abortion does the power of the state violate the liberty interest protected by the Due Process Clause.

FACTS: After the Pennsylvania (D) legislature enacted the Abortion Control Act of 1982, Planned Parenthood (P) challenged five of the provisions. The disputed provisions required that a woman give informed consent to an abortion, requiring a twenty-four-hour delay to review the information given to her, mandated the informed consent of one parent for a minor to obtain an abortion, but provided for a judicial bypass of such consent, required that a married woman notify her husband of her intended abortion, defined a "medical emergency" excusing compliance, and imposed reporting requirements on facilities providing abortion services. The trial court found all five provisions unconstitutional. The court of appeals reversed, upholding all the provisions, except the one requiring husband notification. Planned Parenthood (P) appealed.

ISSUE: Does the power of the state violate the liberty interest protected by the Due Process Clause only where state regulation imposes an undue burden on a woman's ability to procure an abortion?

HOLDING AND DECISION: (O'Connor, J.) Yes. Only where state regulation imposes an undue burden on a woman's ability to procure an abortion does the power of the state violate the liberty interest protected by the Due Process Clause. An undue burden exists, and therefore a provision of law is invalid, if its purpose or effect is to place a substantial obstacle in the path of a woman seeking an abortion before the fetus attains viability. As construed by the court of appeals, the medical emergency definition imposes no undue burden on a woman's abortion right. In addition, the informed consent requirement, along with the twenty-four-hour waiting period, cannot be considered a substantial obstacle to a woman's obtaining an abortion and does not, therefore, constitute an undue burden on that right. However, the spousal notification requirement is likely to prevent a significant number of women who may be victims of spousal abuse from obtaining an abortion. It is an undue burden and is therefore invalid. But a state may require a minor seeking an abortion to obtain the consent of a parent or guardian, provided that there is an adequate judicial bypass procedure. Finally, all the recordkeeping and reporting requirements of the statute, except that relating to spousal notice, are constitutional. Affirmed in part, reversed in part.

CONCURRENCE AND DISSENT: (Stevens, J.) The state (D) may not promote a theological or sectarian interest. A woman's decision to terminate her pregnancy is a matter of conscience. Serious questions arise when a state attempts to persuade a woman to choose childbirth over abortion. A state may promote its preferences by funding childbirth, by creating alternatives to abortion, and by espousing the virtues of family. But it must respect the individual's freedom to make such judgments. The challenged provisions of the Pennsylvania (D) statute are thus unconstitutional.

CONCURRENCE AND DISSENT: (Blackmun, J.) The Constitution and decisions of this Court require that a state's abortion restrictions be subjected to the strictest of judicial scrutiny. Under this standard, the Pennsylvania (D) statute's provisions must be invalidated. Compelled continuation of a pregnancy deprives a woman of the right to make her own decision about reproduction and family planning — critical life choices deemed central to the right to privacy. By restricting the right to terminate pregnancies, the state (D) conscripts women's bodies into its service, forcing women to continue their pregnancies, suffer the pains of childbirth, and in most instances, provide years of maternal care. The Chief Justice's criticism of Roe follows from his stunted conception of individual liberty.

CONCURRENCE AND DISSENT: (Scalia, J.) The states may, if they wish, permit abortion-on-demand, but the Constitution does not require them to do so. Applying the rational basis test, the Pennsylvania (D) statute should be upheld in its entirety. The joint opinion's undue burden standard is inherently manipulable and will prove hopelessly unworkable in practice.

Continued on next page.

EDITOR'S ANALYSIS: Many hoped that with its decision in this case the Court would overrule its holding in Roe v. Wade. However, the plurality stated that the essential holding of Roe should be retained and once again reaffirmed. While the plurality rejected Roe's trimester framework for the undue burden standard, it retained Roe's viability test. The Court noted that its obligation was to define the liberty of all, not to mandate the justices' own moral code. This case was unusual in that three justices — O'Connor, Kennedy, and Souter — took part in writing the plurality opinion.

QUICKNOTES

AMICUS CURIAE - A third party, not a party to the action, who submits a brief to the court containing information for the court's consideration in reaching a determination.

STARE DECISIS - Doctrine whereby courts follow legal precedent unless there is good cause for departure.

DE MINIMIS - Insignificant; trivial; not of sufficient significance to resort to legal action.

SUI GENERIS - Peculiar to its own type or class.

IPSO FACTO - by the fact itself.

NOTES:

IN RE BABY M.

Natural father (P) v. Surrogate mother (D)

N.J. Super. Ct. Ch. Div., 525 A.2d 1128 (1987), rev'd, 537 A.2d 1227 (1988).

NATURE OF CASE: Complaint seeking enforcement of a surrogate-parenting contract.

FACT SUMMARY: The Sterns (P) commenced suit seeking to compel enforcement of a surrogate-parenting contract they had entered into with Mrs. Whitehead (D).

CONCISE RULE OF LAW: Under a surrogate-parenting contract, once conception occurs, the parties' rights in respect to the child are fixed, and may only be altered upon a demonstration that such modification is in the best interests of the child.

FACTS: In 1986, Mr. Stern (P) entered into a surrogate parenting contract with Mr. and Mrs. Whitehead (D). The contract stated that Mrs. Whitehead (D) was to attempt conception of a child by artificial insemination, carry the child to term, deliver the baby, and subsequently surrender the child to Mr. Stern (P), relinquishing all of her parental rights. Mr. Stern (P) would pay all of Mrs. Whitehead's (D) medical expenses as well as an additional $10,000 in consideration of the performance of her duties under the contract. Mrs. Whitehead (D) gave birth to a baby girl. She failed to surrender the child to Mr. Stern (P) pursuant to the contract. Mr. and Mrs. Stern (P) filed an ex parte application for an order to show cause why the court should not issue an order for summary judgment to enforce the contract. The Sterns (P) filed a verified complaint seeking to enforce the contract, compel the surrender of the child, restrain the Whitehead's (D) from interfering with the Stern's (P) custody of the child, terminate Mrs. Whitehead's (D) parental rights, and permit Mrs. Stern (P) to adopt the child.

ISSUE: Under a surrogate-parenting contract, once conception occurs, are the parties' rights in respect to the child fixed, only to be altered upon a demonstration that such modification is in the best interests of the child?

HOLDING AND DECISION: (Sorkow, J.) Yes. Under a surrogate-parenting contract, once conception occurs the parties' rights in respect to the child are fixed, and may only be altered upon a demonstration that such modification is in the best interests of the child. The Whiteheads (D) argued that the surrogate-parenting contract was unconscionable. The Whiteheads (D), however, failed to sustain their burden of showing that overreaching or disproportionate bargaining resulted in an agreement that was unfair to them. The terms of the contract were known to Mrs. Whitehead (D), who had prior experience with surrogacy contracts. The Whiteheads (D) further argued that the contract was illusory on the basis that there was no mutuality of obligation. That argument fails as well. While Mrs.

Whitehead (D) assumed the risk of pregnancy, Mr. Stern (P) assumed the risk that the child be born abnormally. In order to compel the specific performance of a surrogacy contract, the court must first consider the best interests of the child. This determination requires the court to consider: (1) whether the child was wanted or planned for; (2) the emotional stability of the persons in the home environment; (3) the families' stability; (4) the capacity of the adults to recognize and respond to the child's needs; (5) the families' attitudes regarding education; (6) the individuals' capacities to make rational decisions; (7) the individuals' capacities to promote the child's health; (8) the individuals' capacities to explain the circumstances of the child's birth; and (9) the ability of the individuals to assist the child in coping with his or her life. A weighing of these factors results in the conclusion that it is in the best interests of the child that the court specifically enforce the surrogate-parenting contract and award custody to Mr. Stern (P).

EDITOR'S ANALYSIS: The opinion of the trial court in the present case was subsequently overruled by the New Jersey Supreme Court. That court held that the contract was invalid in contravention of state law. Furthermore, the contract violated the public interest favoring children being raised by their natural parents. The court treated the present case as a dispute between two natural parents, Mr. Stern (P) and Mrs. Whitehead (D), awarding custody to Mr. Stern (P) and granting visitation rights to Mrs. Whitehead (D). Other jurisdictions have reached similar conclusions in dealing with the enforcement of surrogate-parenting contracts.

QUICKNOTES

EX PARTE APPLICATION - A proceeding commenced by the application of one party, without providing any opposing parties with notice, or which is uncontested by an adverse party.

NOTES:

FERGUSON v. CITY OF CHARLESTON
Pregnant women (P) v. City (D)
532 U.S. 67 (2001).

NATURE OF CASE: Certiorari review of suspicionless search case.

FACT SUMMARY: Ferguson (P) and several other pregnant women were subjected to drug screens of their urine by Medical University of South Carolina (hereinafter, MUSC). MUSC gave results of positive urine screens to local prosecutors in the City of Charleston (D). Ferguson (P) challenged the constitutionality of the searches. The Supreme Court of the United States granted certiorari review.

CONCISE RULE OF LAW: Screening the urine of pregnant women for drugs in order to provide for the safety of the fetus does not constitute a "special need" divorced from the purpose of law enforcement where the primary goal of the search is to use its fruits to coerce the subjects of the search into treatment through the threat of law enforcement.

FACTS: Ferguson (P) and several other pregnant women were suspected of using narcotics, while pregnant, by the staff of MUSC. The hospital had developed a urine screening policy whereby it screened the urine of pregnant women suspected of using narcotics in accordance with a chain of custody procedure so that it could ultimately provide the results to law enforcement for the purpose of conducting a criminal prosecution. The goal of the program was to preserve the health of the unborn fetuses and to help rehabilitate the expectant mothers. Essentially, the program employed the threat of prosecution to coerce the mothers into treatment. Ferguson (P) challenged the constitutionality of the search in the District Court. The District Court rejected the City of Charleston's (D) defense that the searches were constitutional because they were justified by non-law enforcement purposes. The Court of Appeals disagreed with the District Court and found that the searches were reasonable as a matter of law because protection of unborn children constituted a "special need" that justifies the search policy. The Supreme Court of the United States granted certiorari review of that particular issue.

ISSUE: Does screening the urine of pregnant women for narcotics and providing positive results to law enforcement, for the purpose of protecting the unborn children and coercing the mothers into treatment, constitute a "special need" divorced from the purpose of law enforcement?

HOLDING AND DECISION: (Stevens, J.) No. In prior cases we have held that suspicionless, non-consensual searches may be constitutional, in exceptional circumstances, if the search policy is implemented in order to serve a non-law enforcement purpose. We refer to these cases as "special-needs" cases because the program at issue involved a purpose divorced from law

enforcement that served a "special need." In deciding those cases, we employed a balancing test weighing the intrusion on the individual's interest against the "special need" supporting the search program at issue. The invasion of privacy in this case is significantly greater than the invasion at issue in prior cases. Additionally, those cases involved a purpose that was completely divorced from the state's general interest in law enforcement. What distinguishes this case is that the purpose of the program is to disseminate the results of the urine screening to law enforcement. MUSC intended to coerce mothers into treatment with the threat of criminal prosecution. Although law enforcement was the means the hospital intended to use in order to help mothers abstain from drugs, the program is intertwined with the general objective of law enforcement and is not sufficiently divorced from it. Accordingly, we find that the searches at issue here do not fall into the "special-needs" doctrine and were in violation of the Fourth Amendment rights of the expectant mothers.

DISSENT: (Scalia, J.) We disagree with the majority's Fourth Amendment analysis because we think that urine screening does not constitute a search. We do not regard urine as a personal effect and, therefore, we do not think the protections of the Fourth Amendment extend to urine testing. Assuming, for the sake of argument, that urine is a personal effect, we believe that the expectant mothers in this case consented to the search at issue because it was not extracted from them forcibly. The search was not unreasonable, and, therefore the "special-needs" doctrine is irrelevant. However, assuming, as the majority does, that there was a search and said search was unreasonable, the "special-needs" doctrine would be applicable here. The District Court found that the program's purpose was to protect unborn children. The findings of fact of the lower court are binding upon us. Accordingly, the majority should have found that these searches were lawful under the "special-needs" doctrine.

EDITOR'S ANALYSIS: The majority focused on the distinction between this case and the "special-needs" line of cases. The primary distinction the majority saw between that line of cases and *Ferguson* is that in *Ferguson*, the testing was done with the intent of providing the results to law enforcement and using the threat of criminal prosecution to urge mothers into rehabilitation programs. Had the dissent's position prevailed, an entire class of women would have been deprived of the protections provided by the Fourth Amendment due solely to their capacity to bear children.

CHAPTER 7
ANTI-ESSENTIALISM

QUICK REFERENCE RULES OF LAW

1. **False Universalisms.** A tribal membership ordinance, granting membership to children of male and not female members who marry non-members, is valid and does not constitute a violation of equal protection of tribal laws under the Indian Civil Rights Act. (Martinez v. Santa Clara Pueblo)

2. **The Naturalist Error.** A transsexual who has married a person of his or her former sex cannot be considered that person's spouse because the law sees a person's sex as immutable. (Littleton v. Prange)

3. **The Naturalist Error.** The fact that a man was denied a loan application because he was dressed as a woman is sufficient evidence of sex discrimination to survive a motion to dismiss. (Rosa v. Park West Bank & Trust Co.)

MARTINEZ v. SANTA CLARA PUEBLO
Pueblo member (P) v. Pueblo (D)
402 F. Supp. 5 (D.N.M. 1975), rev'd and remanded, 540 F2.d. 1039 (10th Cir. 1976), rev'd, 436 U.S. 49 (1978).

NATURE OF CASE: Class action suit claiming a tribal ordinance deprived members of the class of their rights of equal protection and due process in violation of the Indian Civil Rights Act (ICRA) and seeking an injunction against the further enforcement of the ordinance.

FACT SUMMARY: Martinez (P) commenced suit against the Santa Clara Pueblo (D) and Governor Lucario Padilla (D), claiming that a tribal ordinance denying membership to the children of female and not male members of the Pueblo who marry non-members violated the Indian Civil Rights Act, 25 U.S.C. § 1302(8), by denying those persons equal protection and due process of law.

CONCISE RULE OF LAW: A tribal membership ordinance, granting membership to children of male and not female members who marry non-members, is valid and does not constitute a violation of equal protection of tribal laws under the Indian Civil Rights Act.

FACTS: Julia Martinez (P), a member of the Santa Clara Pueblo (D), married a non-member of the Pueblo (D). In 1968, Congress enacted the Indian Civil Rights Act (ICRA) in order to guarantee the more significant civil rights to Indians residing on reservations. The Santa Clara Pueblo (D) enacted an ordinance in 1939 stating that children born to male members of the Pueblo (D) who had married non-members would be members of the Pueblo (D). The ordinance denied membership to children of female members of the Pueblo (D) who married non-members. Martinez' (P) children were not recognized as Pueblo (D) members under that ordinance. Martinez (P) brought suit as the representative of the class consisting of all female members of the Santa Clara Pueblo (D) who had married non-members of the pueblo. Her daughter, Audrey (P), brought suit as a representative of the class consisting of all children born to such marriages who are not recognized as members of the Pueblo (D). They both claimed that the ordinance violated the ICRA, which prohibited a tribal government from denying any persons within its jurisdiction their rights of equal protection and due process. They also sought an injunction against the further enforcement of the ordinance.

ISSUE: Is a tribal membership ordinance, granting membership to children of male and not female members who marry non-members, valid and does not constitute a violation of equal protection of tribal laws under the Indian Civil Rights Act?

HOLDING AND DECISION: (Mechem, J.) Yes. A tribal membership ordinance, granting membership to children of male and not female members who marry non-members, is valid and does not constitute a violation of equal protection of tribal laws under the Indian Civil Rights Act. Members of the Pueblo (D) are afforded three distinct rights, including political rights, land use rights, and the right to continue residing on the Pueblo (D). Martinez (P) claimed that the ordinance placed a restriction on her rights and rights which she could grant to her children as Pueblo (D) members. The Pueblo (D) contended that the ordinance sought to codify traditional custom, since the classification of children of mixed marriages traditionally followed patrilineal lines. The Supreme Court has held that Indian tribes are unique entities entitled to sovereignty over their members and territory. However, the sovereign power of the Indian Tribes is subject to regulation by Congress. In the absence of Congressional limitations, the tribe has the authority to make decisions regarding its membership. The determinative issue is to what extent the ICRA regulates such determinations. Courts have held that the equal protection guarantee under § 1302(8) is not the same as that under the federal Constitution. Rather, that clause must be construed within the context of tribal law and tradition. That section requires, at the very least, that tribal law be applied equitably and not arbitrarily and that procedural due process must be afforded in denying or granting certain benefits. Based on these considerations, § 1302(8) should not be interpreted as invalidating a tribal membership ordinance based on membership criteria customarily utilized by the tribe. Thus, the 1939 Ordinance did not deny Martinez (P) equal protection of the law in violation of the ICRA.

EDITOR'S ANALYSIS: The court of appeals subsequently reversed the present case, holding that the ordinance constituted an impermissible gender-based classification that was not justified by a substantial tribal interest. The Supreme Court granted certiorari. The Court subsequently reversed the court of appeals' judgment, not on the merits but on the basis that suits against Indian tribes are generally prohibited by their sovereign immunity. Since Congress has the absolute power to regulate in respect to the Indian tribes, the Court held that in the absence of an express revocation of such immunity, a federal court does not have jurisdiction to resolve suits brought against an Indian tribe or one of its officers.

QUICKNOTES

INDIAN CIVIL RIGHTS ACT - prohibits a tribal government from denying to any persons within its jurisdiction the equal protection of its laws or depriving any person of liberty or property without due process of law.

LITTLETON v. PRANGE

Transsexual (P) v. Doctor (D)

9 S.W.3d 223 (1999).

NATURE OF CASE: Appeal of summary judgment.

FACT SUMMARY: Littleton (P), a transsexual who married a man, sued Prange (D) for the wrongful death of her husband. Prange (D) moved for summary judgment claiming that, as a transsexual, Littleton (P) could not be the surviving spouse of a man and, therefore, had no standing to bring a wrongful death action. The trial court ruled in favor of Prange (D) and Littleton (P) filed this appeal.

CONCISE RULE OF LAW: A transsexual who has married a person of his or her former sex cannot be considered that person's spouse because the law sees a person's sex as immutable.

FACTS: Littleton (P) was born with full male genitalia. However, she knew, from the age of three, that she was a female. By age 17 she had sought out a surgeon to do a sex reassignment surgery. At 23, Littleton (P) was officially a woman. She had female genitalia and her birth certificate was amended to reflect her true sex. Littleton (P) married a man in 1989 and he died in 1996. As the surviving spouse of her husband, Littleton (P) brought a wrongful death action against the doctor, Prange (D). Prange (D) filed a motion for summary judgment claiming that Littleton (P) did not have standing to bring a wrongful death action because she, as a man, could not be the spouse of another man. The trial court granted Prange's (D) motion for summary judgment. Littleton (P) filed this appeal.

ISSUE: Is a transsexual who marries a person of his or her former sex legally married to that person?

HOLDING AND DECISION: (Hardberger, C.J.) No. The legislature has not addressed the issue of marriages between a transsexual and a person of his or her former sex. It is not for us to make law, but rather, to interpret law that already exists. Littleton (P) was born a male. Her original birth certificate clearly stated that fact. Though she had the certificate amended based on a statute entitling her to do so if her birth certificate was "inaccurate," we do not believe the legislature intended that term to include the present situation. At birth, Littleton (P) was a male, and her birth certificate truly and accurately reflects that fact. We find that the law recognizes her as a male to this day. Accordingly, we find that she could not be the spouse of a male and, therefore, does not have standing to bring a wrongful death action as his surviving spouse.

CONCURRENCE: (Angelini, J.) I agree with the majority, but I note that even when courts consider biological factors alone, there will still be cases in which a person's gender is ambiguous.

DISSENT: (Lopez, J.) I disagree with the majority because I think this case is inappropriate for summary judgment. The issue of whether or not Littleton (P) is a surviving spouse is a question of fact for a jury.

EDITOR'S ANALYSIS: It is interesting that the majority refers to Littleton (P) throughout the case as though she were a woman only to find that she is a man. This contradiction reflects the difficulties courts have in dealing with transsexuality. There is no legal language or frame of reference for understanding it.

NOTES:

ROSA v. PARK WEST BANK & TRUST CO.

Transvestite (P) v. Bank (D)

214 F.3d 213 (1st Cir. 2000).

NATURE OF CASE: Appeal of motion to dismiss.

FACT SUMMARY: Rosa (P), a man, went into the Park West Bank & Trust Co. (hereinafter, Bank) (D) dressed as a woman and the teller refused to give him a loan application until he changed his clothing. Rosa (P) sued the Bank (D) for sex discrimination. The Bank (D) filed a 12(b)(6) motion to dismiss and the trial court granted the motion. Rosa (P) filed this appeal.

CONCISE RULE OF LAW: The fact that a man was denied a loan application because he was dressed as a woman is sufficient evidence of sex discrimination to survive a motion to dismiss.

FACTS: Rosa (P), a man, went into the Bank (D) dressed as a woman. When he requested a loan application, the teller asked him for identification. Rosa (P) provided three forms of identification in which he appeared in more traditionally male attire. The teller informed Rosa (P) that she would not give him a loan application until he went home and changed into more masculine attire. Rosa (P) filed a claim for discrimination under the Equal Credit Opportunity Act. The Bank (D) filed a motion to dismiss. The trial court granted the motion on the basis that the teller had denied Rosa (P) a credit application because of the manner in which he was dressed, not based on his sex. Rosa (P) filed this appeal.

ISSUE: Is evidence of a teller's refusal to give a man a loan application telling him to "go home and change," where the man was dressed as a woman, sufficient evidence of sex discrimination to survive a motion to dismiss?

HOLDING AND DECISION: (Lynch, J.) Yes. The evidence in this case is not developed enough for the trial court to have determined that it should be dismissed for failure to state a claim upon which relief can be granted. It is not clear why the teller refused to give Rosa (P) an application until he changed. It could be that the teller assumed that Rosa (P) was gay because he was dressed as a woman and refused to give him an application for that reason. If that were the case, the statute at issue would not apply because it does not address discrimination based on sexual orientation. Another possibility is that the teller would have treated a woman similarly situated as Rosa (P), that is a woman who dresses like a man, differently. In that case, Rosa (P) would have a successful claim of sex discrimination. The evidence is not developed enough to be the basis of a determination that Rosa (P) did not have a claim of sex discrimination. The trial court erred in granting the motion to dismiss.

EDITOR'S ANALYSIS: The Court indicated in dicta that if the Bank (D) can show that the teller merely discriminated on the basis of what Rosa (P) was wearing, that would not be sufficient to support a claim of sex discrimination. Rosa (P), instead, must show that the Bank (D) would have treated a similarly situated woman differently. That is, Rosa (P) must present evidence that the Bank (D) would have treated a woman who dresses as a man differently—a seemingly impossible burden.

NOTES:

GLOSSARY
COMMON LATIN WORDS AND PHRASES ENCOUNTERED IN THE LAW

A FORTIORI: Because one fact exists or has been proven, therefore a second fact that is related to the first fact must also exist.

A PRIORI: From the cause to the effect. A term of logic used to denote that when one generally accepted truth is shown to be a cause, another particular effect must necessarily follow.

AB INITIO: From the beginning; a condition which has existed throughout, as in a marriage which was void ab initio.

ACTUS REUS: The wrongful act; in criminal law, such action sufficient to trigger criminal liability.

AD VALOREM: According to value; an ad valorem tax is imposed upon an item located within the taxing jurisdiction calculated by the value of such item.

AMICUS CURIAE: Friend of the court. Its most common usage takes the form of an amicus curiae brief, filed by a person who is not a party to an action but is nonetheless allowed to offer an argument supporting his legal interests.

ARGUENDO: In arguing. A statement, possibly hypothetical, made for the purpose of argument, is one made arguendo.

BILL QUIA TIMET: A bill to quiet title (establish ownership) to real property.

BONA FIDE: True, honest, or genuine. May refer to a person's legal position based on good faith or lacking notice of fraud (such as a bona fide purchaser for value) or to the authenticity of a particular document (such as a bona fide last will and testament).

CAUSA MORTIS: With approaching death in mind. A gift causa mortis is a gift given by a party who feels certain that death is imminent.

CAVEAT EMPTOR: Let the buyer beware. This maxim is reflected in the rule of law that a buyer purchases at his own risk because it is his responsibility to examine, judge, test, and otherwise inspect what he is buying.

CERTIORARI: A writ of review. Petitions for review of a case by the United States Supreme Court are most often done by means of a writ of certiorari.

CONTRA: On the other hand. Opposite. Contrary to.

CORAM NOBIS: Before us; writs of error directed to the court that originally rendered the judgment.

CORAM VOBIS: Before you; writs of error directed by an appellate court to a lower court to correct a factual error.

CORPUS DELICTI: The body of the crime; the requisite elements of a crime amounting to objective proof that a crime has been committed.

CUM TESTAMENTO ANNEXO, ADMINISTRATOR (ADMINISTRATOR C.T.A.): With will annexed; an administrator c.t.a. settles an estate pursuant to a will in which he is not appointed.

DE BONIS NON, ADMINISTRATOR (ADMINISTRATOR D.B.N.): Of goods not administered; an administrator d.b.n. settles a partially settled estate.

DE FACTO: In fact; in reality; actually. Existing in fact but not officially approved or engendered.

DE JURE: By right; lawful. Describes a condition that is legitimate "as a matter of law," in contrast to the term "de facto," which connotes something existing in fact but not legally sanctioned or authorized. For example, de facto segregation refers to segregation brought about by housing patterns, etc., whereas de jure segregation refers to segregation created by law.

DE MINIMUS: Of minimal importance; insignificant; a trifle; not worth bothering about.

DE NOVO: Anew; a second time; afresh. A trial de novo is a new trial held at the appellate level as if the case originated there and the trial at a lower level had not taken place.

DICTA: Generally used as an abbreviated form of obiter dicta, a term describing those portions of a judicial opinion incidental or not necessary to resolution of the specific question before the court. Such nonessential statements and remarks are not considered to be binding precedent.

DUCES TECUM: Refers to a particular type of writ or subpoena requesting a party or organization to produce certain documents in their possession.

EN BANC: Full bench. Where a court sits with all justices present rather than the usual quorum.

EX PARTE: For one side or one party only. An ex parte proceeding is one undertaken for the benefit of only one party, without notice to, or an appearance by, an adverse party.

EX POST FACTO: After the fact. An ex post facto law is a law that retroactively changes the consequences of a prior act.

EX REL.: Abbreviated form of the term ex relatione, meaning, upon relation or information. When the state brings an action in which it has no interest against an individual at the instigation of one who has a private interest in the matter.

FORUM NON CONVENIENS: Inconvenient forum. Although a court may have jurisdiction over the case, the action should be tried in a more conveniently located court, one to which parties and witnesses may more easily travel, for example.

GUARDIAN AD LITEM: A guardian of an infant as to litigation, appointed to represent the infant and pursue his/her rights.

HABEAS CORPUS: You have the body. The modern writ of habeas corpus is a writ directing that a person (body) being detained (such as a prisoner) be brought before the court so that the legality of his detention can be judicially ascertained.

IN CAMERA: In private, in chambers. When a hearing is held before a judge in his chambers or when all spectators are excluded from the courtroom.

IN FORMA PAUPERIS: In the manner of a pauper. A party who proceeds in forma pauperis because of his poverty is one who is allowed to bring suit without liability for costs.

INFRA: Below, under. A word referring the reader to a later part of a book. (The opposite of supra.)

IN LOCO PARENTIS: In the place of a parent.

IN PARI DELICTO: Equally wrong; a court of equity will not grant requested relief to an applicant who is in pari delicto, or as much at fault in the transactions giving rise to the controversy as is the opponent of the applicant.

IN PARI MATERIA: On like subject matter or upon the same matter. Statutes relating to the same person or things are said to be in pari materia. It is a general rule of statutory construction that such statutes should be construed together, i.e., looked at as if they together constituted one law.

IN PERSONAM: Against the person. Jurisdiction over the person of an individual.

IN RE: In the matter of. Used to designate a proceeding involving an estate or other property.

IN REM: A term that signifies an action against the res, or thing. An action in rem is basically one that is taken directly against property, as distinguished from an action in personam, i.e., against the person.

INTER ALIA: Among other things. Used to show that the whole of a statement, pleading, list, statute, etc., has not been set forth in its entirety.

INTER PARTES: Between the parties. May refer to contracts, conveyances or other transactions having legal significance.

INTER VIVOS: Between the living. An inter vivos gift is a gift made by a living grantor, as distinguished from bequests contained in a will, which pass upon the death of the testator.

IPSO FACTO: By the mere fact itself.

JUS: Law or the entire body of law.

LEX LOCI: The law of the place; the notion that the rights of parties to a legal proceeding are governed by the law of the place where those rights arose.

MALUM IN SE: Evil or wrong in and of itself; inherently wrong. This term describes an act that is wrong by its very nature, as opposed to one which would not be wrong but for the fact that there is a specific legal prohibition against it (malum prohibitum).

MALUM PROHIBITUM: Wrong because prohibited, but not inherently evil. Used to describe something that is wrong because it is expressly forbidden by law but that is not in and of itself evil, e.g., speeding.

MANDAMUS: We command. A writ directing an official to take a certain action.

MENS REA: A guilty mind; a criminal intent. A term used to signify the mental state that accompanies a crime or other prohibited act. Some crimes require only a general mens rea (general intent to do the prohibited act), but others, like assault with intent to murder, require the existence of a specific mens rea.

MODUS OPERANDI: Method of operating; generally refers to the manner or style of a criminal in committing crimes, admissible in appropriate cases as evidence of the identity of a defendant.

NEXUS: A connection to.

NISI PRIUS: A court of first impression. A nisi prius court is one where issues of fact are tried before a judge or jury.

N.O.V. (NON OBSTANTE VEREDICTO): Notwithstanding the verdict. A judgment n.o.v. is a judgment given in favor of one party despite the fact that a verdict was returned in favor of the other party, the justification being that the verdict either had no reasonable support in fact or was contrary to law.

NUNC PRO TUNC: Now for then. This phrase refers to actions that may be taken and will then have full retroactive effect.

PENDENTE LITE: Pending the suit; pending litigation underway.

PER CAPITA: By head; beneficiaries of an estate, if they take in equal shares, take per capita.

PER CURIAM: By the court; signifies an opinion ostensibly written "by the whole court" and with no identified author.

PER SE: By itself, in itself; inherently.

PER STIRPES: By representation. Used primarily in the law of wills to describe the method of distribution where a person, generally because of death, is unable to take that which is left to him by the will of another, and therefore his heirs divide such property between them rather than take under the will individually.

PRIMA FACIE: On its face, at first sight. A prima facie case is one that is sufficient on its face, meaning that the evidence supporting it is adequate to establish the case until contradicted or overcome by other evidence.

PRO TANTO: For so much; as far as it goes. Often used in eminent domain cases when a property owner receives partial payment for his land without prejudice to his right to bring suit for the full amount he claims his land to be worth.

QUANTUM MERUIT: As much as he deserves. Refers to recovery based on the doctrine of unjust enrichment in those cases in which a party has rendered valuable services or furnished materials that were accepted and enjoyed by another under circumstances that would reasonably notify the recipient that the rendering party expected to be paid. In essence, the law implies a contract to pay the reasonable value of the services or materials furnished.

QUASI: Almost like; as if; nearly. This term is essentially used to signify that one subject or thing is almost analogous to another but that material differences between them do exist. For example, a quasi-criminal proceeding is one that is not strictly criminal but shares enough of the same characteristics to require some of the same safeguards (e.g., procedural due process must be followed in a parol hearing).

QUID PRO QUO: Something for something. In contract law, the consideration, something of value, passed between the parties to render the contract binding.

RES GESTAE: Things done; in evidence law, this principle justifies the admission of a statement that would otherwise be hearsay when it is made so closely to the event in question as to be said to be a part of it, or with such spontaneity as not to have the possibility of falsehood.

RES IPSA LOQUITUR: The thing speaks for itself. This doctrine gives rise to a rebuttable presumption of negligence when the instrumentality causing the injury was within the exclusive control of the defendant, and the injury was one that does not normally occur unless a person has been negligent.

RES JUDICATA: A matter adjudged. Doctrine which provides that once a court of competent jurisdiction has rendered a final judgment or decree on the merits, that judgment or decree is conclusive upon the parties to the case and prevents them from engaging in any other litigation on the points and issues determined therein.

RESPONDEAT SUPERIOR: Let the master reply. This doctrine holds the master liable for the wrongful acts of his servant (or the principal for his agent) in those cases in which the servant (or agent) was acting within the scope of his authority at the time of the injury.

STARE DECISIS: To stand by or adhere to that which has been decided. The common law doctrine of stare decisis attempts to give security and certainty to the law by following the policy that once a principle of law as applicable to a certain set of facts has been set forth in a decision, it forms a precedent which will subsequently be followed, even though a different decision might be made were it the first time the question had arisen. Of course, stare decisis is not an inviolable principle and is departed from in instances where there is good cause (e.g., considerations of public policy led the Supreme Court to disregard prior decisions sanctioning segregation).

SUPRA: Above. A word referring a reader to an earlier part of a book.

ULTRA VIRES: Beyond the power. This phrase is most commonly used to refer to actions taken by a corporation that are beyond the power or legal authority of the corporation.

ADDENDUM OF FRENCH DERIVATIVES

IN PAIS: Not pursuant to legal proceedings.

CHATTEL: Tangible personal property.

CY PRES: Doctrine permitting courts to apply trust funds to purposes not expressed in the trust but necessary to carry out the settlor's intent.

PER AUTRE VIE: For another's life; in property law, an estate may be granted that will terminate upon the death of someone other than the grantee.

PROFIT A PRENDRE: A license to remove minerals or other produce from land.

VOIR DIRE: Process of questioning jurors as to their predispositions about the case or parties to a proceeding in order to identify those jurors displaying bias or prejudice.

REV 1-95

CASENOTE LEGAL BRIEFS